REMEMBER- POSITIVE EXPECTATIONS HELP TO BRING POSITIVE CHANGES IN YOUR LIFE.

Eric R. Jackson 2017

EXPECTATIONS

THEY CAN MAKE YOU OR BREAK YOU

ERIC RONALD JACKSON

WestBow Press books may be ordered through booksellers or by contacting:

WestBow Press
A Division of Thomas Nelson & Zondervan
1663 Liberty Drive
Bloomington, IN 47403
www.westbowpress.com
1 (866) 928-1240

ISBN: 978-1-5127-4549-8 (sc)
ISBN: 978-1-5127-4550-4 (hc)
ISBN: 978-1-5127-4548-1 (e)

Library of Congress Control Number: 2016909518

Print information available on the last page.

WestBow Press rev. date: 6/20/2016

Contents

Foreword

It is truly an honor to review the writing on expectations from the author Mr. Eric Jackson. I have known Mr. Jackson for over thirteen years. Mr. Jackson is one of several overachievers who came from this wonderful community. Springfield Baptist Church is where he received his training.

Mr. Jackson is well versed in the scripture and has years of experience in dealing with the subject matter presented in his book. I had the opportunity to read the manuscript several times. Each time I read his manuscript I found something I can use to assist me in my Christian walk. The book is profound and consistent with different life experiences. The author's point of view adheres to Christian values in understanding scripture and applying it to everyday life. He gives his audiences insight with the support of his Christian beliefs. Mr. Jackson's work is for readers of all ages.

I would have to say that the author put quality time in this work and it is a must-read. We all are expecting something from everything we do in life. This book reveals this in the author's work.

Rev. Theodore T. Brown, DD
Pastor of Springfield Baptist Church
Meherrin, Virginia

Preface

Shortly after the Lord helped me publish my first book, *A New Life: The Only Way to Win,*[1] in 1996, something caused me to start thinking about another book. Every now and then when a thought came to me concerning expectations, I would jot down the thought and include a brief explanation of that thought. I don't know why I delayed writing this book. Maybe it was because I expected better results from the distribution of the first book and got discouraged. Also, the book required a lot of work and cost a lot to publish and distribute.

I must say there was one young man who inspired me, Rev. Dana Farmer Sr., Co-Pastor of Hills Avenue Baptist Church in Atlanta, Georgia, and a member of The Abyssinian Baptist Church of New York City, where he resides. I had not met him in person, but he purchased over one hundred copies of my first book and we have developed a good friendship over the years. I did not expect his actions beforehand.

After I was a trustee at my church for over twenty years, my resignation gave me more available time to do other things. My resignation took away some of the excuses I had been giving myself for not spending more time in writing this book. Note, I do not consider myself a writer of books. After expanding the thoughts I had jotted down about expectations and arranging them in somewhat of a logical order, my interest in publishing another book increased.

Expectations: They Can Make You or Break You is a book based on my experiences and my teaching of the Holy Bible over many years.

Therefore, the book has many references to verses in the Bible. However, Christians, or others of any religious or nonreligious groups, are not the only ones who have expectations—we all have them.

Rev. Dan Reiland says, "We are all managing unmet expectations. How you deal with that fact can make you or break you." He also says the following:

- "Unmet expectations in your marriage can be very frustrating.
- Unmet expectations with your friends can be disappointing.
- Unmet expectations financially can be a real source of conflict."[2]

By reading this book, hopefully you will become more aware of—and get a better understanding of—expectations, especially the importance of positive expectations and what you may experience from negative expectations. Of course this book does not include all expectations. By discussing expectations in a few topics, you may be able to expand this knowledge to topics of interest to you; for example, what you expect from your family, your spouse, your children, your boss, your doctor, your car, your lawyer, your government, your political party representative, your president, your leader, etc.

Acknowledgments

This book would not have been possible without the inspiration, guidance, patience, wisdom, and other wonderful qualities of God the Father, God the Son, and God the Holy Spirit. Therefore, I thank them for all they did to make this book possible.

Thanks to Rev. Theodore Brown, DD, pastor of the Springfield Baptist Church, Meherrin, Virginia, for being willing to review the manuscript and provide helpful comments. He did this for me even though he had a large workload.

Thanks to my wife, Celestine, who has been my helpmate for over fifty-four years.

Thanks to Virgil Tyler, the husband of my daughter, Cheryl, for volunteering to review the manuscript. He also had many other things he could have chosen to do instead.

Also thanks to the following people for giving me permission to use some of their information in this book:

Livia Bardin, MSW, and the International Cultic Studies Association for their comments and use of quotes from Ms. Bardin's book *Starting Out in Mainstream America*.

Mr. Dave Fleet Sr., vice president in Edelman's Toronto office.

Rev. Dan Reiland, executive pastor, 12 Stone Church, Lawrenceville, Georgia.

Ms. Sheri Stritof, writer for About Relationships, and widow and widower support expert.

Thanks to the Westbow Press staff for assistance and guidance in completing the publishing process of this book.

Thanks to all of you who purchased this book. May you find something in it that will help you understand expectations better and inspire you to help others with their expectations.

CHAPTER 1

Introduction

As we go through life each day, we do something so routine that we don't even think about it. It is almost like breathing, thinking, or walking—we expect. We expect the sun to rise each morning. We expect to wake up the next morning, especially if we are healthy. We expect our prayers to be answered. We expect God to do what He promised. We expect particular results from our decisions. We have expectations for our families. However, all of us may have different levels of expectations, because different people may expect different things from the same source.

Our expectations can range from high to low (or seemingly no expectations), important to meaningless, substantial to trivial, conscious to unconscious, etc. Mr. Dave Fleet said in his article "Expectations Can Make or Break You" that "expectations are critical."[3]

If you were to ask a group of people the following questions, each question could have as many answers as there were people in the group. Also, if the circumstances, experiences, and knowledge of a person change over time, his or her answers may change.

- What do you expect from life?
- What do you expect when you sit in a chair?

- What do you expect from your wife or husband, children, grandchildren, boyfriend or girlfriend, mother, father, or friend?
- What do you expect from your car, house, or clothing?
- What do you expect from your church leaders, barber, teacher, beautician, salesperson, or government?
- What do you expect when you pray?
- What do you expect from God?

If we think about our expectations, we may conclude that we expect something, or nothing, from many things ... maybe everything. My conclusion is that *we expect someone or something to perform at a particular level for a particular situation*. This is similar to the definition of *trust—a confident expectation of someone or something.* Trust is a high level of expectation.

When we look at the conclusion again, "we expect someone or something to perform at a particular level for a particular situation," we see that the statement will have the same meaning if we replace "expect" with "believe." Therefore, the use of the word "*expect*" in this book implies confidently believing that an event will occur. With this understanding, the statement could be used to define faith—**faith is a confident expectation that someone or something will perform to a particular level and having enough evidence to believe (or know) that what is expected has a possibility of happening.**

The phrase "particular level" can be understood better by considering a few examples. Most of us do not inspect a chair before we sit in it, provided the chair looks okay. We expect the chair to support our weight when we sit down. Our level of expectation is that the chair will not fall or collapse when we sit in it. However, our level of expectation or confidence will decrease if the chair shakes when we put our hands on it. Levels of expectation will be discussed in more details in chapter 2.

Another example of "particular level" involves my experience with my former fourteen-year-old pickup truck. My desire was to keep the truck until it "fell apart." I waxed it twice a year, so the original paint was still in reasonably good shape; it looked good for a fourteen-year-old truck. I bought a couple of cases of oil and some filters for me to perform oil changes. Changing the oil and filter before the manufacturer's scheduled time probably helped the engine not to use a measurable amount of oil in three thousand miles—after over one hundred thousand miles of operation. During those miles of operation, I was blessed that the truck did not break down while I was on a road trip.

What was my level of expectation for the performance of my truck? Did I have faith in my truck?

The answers are that my levels of expectation and faith were high when the truck was new and decreased as it got older.

As my truck got older, I started evaluating my expectations of it. For example, when it was older, I made this evaluation. Even though the truck did not break down on the road, several repairs would be needed within a few months, and each one would cost more than two hundred dollars. Also, I noticed that some of the plastic parts were deteriorating, which changed my expectations of the truck. So I purchased a new truck. Was faith in my old truck a factor in my buying a new truck? Yes!

My expectations for a truck I own is to provide transportation for at least two hundred miles one way and back without the need of repairs. The need for repairs and the deterioration of the plastic parts made me think the truck would start breaking down on the road. Therefore I did not have a confident expectation that the truck would travel four hundred miles without needing repairs.

So here are answers to the questions above for my level of expectation and having faith in my fourteen-year-old truck. What was my level of expectation?—to provide transportation for at least two hundred miles one way and back without the need of repairs. What is the particular situation?—anytime I was driving it on a two-hundred-mile, or longer, trip. Therefore, the deterioration of the plastic parts and the increased maintenance resulted in my expecting the truck to operate satisfactorily for short trips but not for longer trips—a reduced faith in my truck.

This example indicates that our expectations are influenced by our knowledge (education) and experiences. Consider what we do before we sit in a chair. Our knowledge and/or experiences will cause us to glance, maybe unconsciously, at a chair before sitting in it. If it looks like other chairs we have sat in before, we expect it to support us. If one piece of the chair is bent or broken, our expectation of it to support us decreases, which makes our level of expectation lower. To bring our level of expectation up to the point that we will sit in the chair, we then need confirmation. We may look to see if someone else our size is sitting in a similar chair, or we may slowly and cautiously put our weight on the chair. As we cautiously increase our weight on the chair—without problems—our expectation likewise increases.

To show how knowledge and experience can affect our expectations, consider several examples using a person we will call Judy. For a short background for Judy, let's say she has a loving dad—with whom she has a good relationship. She has had good experiences in her dating relationships. She is not married. However, she has had a bad experience with a male person that most people would have a tendency to trust—say, a pastor of a church.

Example 1—Judy meets a man she has not met before or heard anything about.

Results: Her perceived expectation is probably average for her.

Example 2—Judy meets a man as in Example 1. During her first discussion with him, she learns that he is a pastor.

Results: Her perceived expectation probably drops significantly.

Example 3—Judy meets a man as in Example 2, but he looks like her dad.

Results: Her expectation may drop some but not as much as in Example 2. Her expectation may be influenced by the man's features—since the features remind her of her dad.

Example 4—Judy meets a man as in Example 2. From talking with the man and talking to others who know the man, she learns this pastor is a loving father who cares for and loves people.

Results: Her expectation probably increases significantly. Also, her expectation is probably coming from what she perceived and is based on her knowledge plus experience(s).

Example 5—Judy meets a man as in Example 2, but someone tells her negative things about the pastor.

Results: Her expectation probably drops lower than for Example 2, even if she doesn't know the person who told her the negative things.

There could be many examples for Judy's expectations of men she meets, but hopefully you can get an idea how a person's expectations of someone or something can be influenced by many factors. Therefore, a person's level of expectations is constantly changing as his or her knowledge and experience(s) change.

Expectation Compared to Walking a Straight Line

Consider a person who wants to walk the straightest line from one post to another post located one hundred yards away, assuming there are no obstructions between the two posts. If the person has little knowledge and experience in walking a "straight' line, he may look down near his feet and not at the other pole as he walks. This approach may cause him to wander and never reach the other post. If he looks down close to his feet for a period of time and then occasionally looks up at the other post, he may stray off course but can correct his direction each time he looks up until he reaches the other post. If he keeps his focus on the other post as he walks toward it, we can expect him to walk the straightest line.

These expected results can be likened to different levels, or degrees, of faith in Jesus—no faith, little faith, and great faith. An unsaved person (no faith in Jesus) is like the person who looks down near his feet while he is walking. There is a goal, but he may not reach it, because he is thinking only about himself and does not want to know what is at the destination.

A carnal Christian[4] (little faith) is like the person who knows about the destination and looks at it occasionally to get back on course. He is concerned about things of this life and occasionally looks to the Lord to get back on track. However, he could get so far off track that reaching the destination seems hopeless; but no matter how dim the destination is, he can get back on track. This reminds me of the parable of the lost son (see Luke 15:11–24).

Then there is the mature Christian (great faith in Jesus), who keeps his eyes on the destination—the prize. He may fall down, but he keeps his focus on God. He may endure hardships, but he keeps his focus. He may experience the temptations and trials of this world, but he keeps his focus on God. He would be able to say with confidence something similar to what the apostle Paul said in Romans 8:35–39 (NIV):

> Who shall separate us from the love of Christ? Shall trouble or hardship or persecution or famine or nakedness or danger or sword? As it is written: "For your sake we face death all day long; we are considered as sheep to be slaughtered." No, in all these things we are more than conquerors through him who loved us. For I am convinced that neither death nor life, neither angels nor demons, neither the present nor the future, nor any powers, neither height nor depth, nor anything else in all creation, will be able to separate us from the love of God that is in Christ Jesus our Lord.

Best Source of Expectations

You may have heard the expression "Whom can I trust?" This question is usually asked after a person has lost confidence in another person. It is a good question, one that we should ask ourselves before making decisions to keep from being hurt emotionally, financially, and other similar ways. However, getting satisfactory answers to that question may be difficult.

The best general answer is given in Psalm 118:8–9 (KJV): "It is better to trust in the LORD than to put confidence in man. It is better to trust in the LORD than to put confidence in princes." Why? Because it is hard to know a man; he changes continually. Who knows the thoughts, motives, attitudes, and mind of another person?

Whenever we expect too much or too little from someone or something, we are setting ourselves up for possible hurt or disappointment. For example, if a parent expects performance from a child that is greater than the ability of that child, the parent may get disappointed and the child may receive emotional damage. If a person expects a chair to serve the purpose of a ladder, it is possible the person may get hurt if he uses the chair in that way.

Not only can people expect too much or too little of people and material things, people can expect too much and too little of God. First, let's discuss how someone can expect too much from God.

Suppose someone reads 1 John 5:14–15 (KJV), which says, "And this is the confidence that we have in him, that, if we ask any thing according to his will, he heareth us: And if we know that he hear us, whatsoever we ask, we know that we have the petitions that we desired of him."

With this scripture in mind, and since he believes the Bible, he prays for God to heal a loved one of a physical illness, like cancer. But instead of the loved one getting better, the loved one gets worse and dies. If he did not understand the scripture in 1 John and expected God to answer all of his prayers the way he wanted, he could become frustrated with God. The scripture says if we ask anything according to His will—not anything according to our will only. If it is God's will and purpose for the person to die instead of being healed, the person will die.

Likewise, someone can expect too little of God. I have heard of people saying that God does not have time for them ... or that their problem is too small to ask God for help. They may not realize that God is omniscient (all-knowing), omnipresent (present everywhere), and omnipotent (all-strong)—therefore God is capable of handling all problems from everyone. (Sometimes small problems end up being big problems if they are not resolved when they are small.)

Even though some people realize God is the best source for their expectations, they have a tendency to put their confidence in man. The more wealth people have, the more they tend to trust material things rather than God. If one person is poor and another is wealthy, which one do you think will expect God to help him and which one may be inclined to rely on his wealth for a solution?

Proverbs 3:5–6 (KJV) states, "Trust in the LORD with all thine heart; and lean not unto thine own understanding. In all thy ways acknowledge him, and he shall direct thy paths." In order to trust Him, you must know Him. To know Him you must read and study His Word—the Bible. To understand His Word, you need guidance from the Holy Spirit,[5] directly or from someone inspired by the Holy Spirit.

Positive and Negative Expectations

Your feelings, manner, or position toward a person or thing (attitude) can be positive or negative. Likewise, positive or negative expectations of something or somebody can affect your life.

For example, fear affects many people. Fear can be positive or negative, good or bad. Of course, fear is directly related to a person's expectations of something or somebody. And those expectations are based on that person's basis for believing that what he or she desires has a good possibility of happening. Therefore, the basis of someone's belief is very important.

A few examples can show how the basis of a person's belief can affect his life.

God told Moses to send twelve men to explore the land of Canaan, which He was giving to the Israelites. So Moses chose one man from each tribe and sent them on a mission to get some information for him. One thing the men were to do was to see what the land was like and whether the people who lived there were strong or weak, few or many (see Numbers 13:1–2, 18).

When the men returned with their report, ten of them said the land flowed with milk and honey, but the men in the land were powerful and the cities were fortified and many. The ten men said not only were the men there powerful, they were large. Their size made the ten men consider themselves (the ten) to be like grasshoppers. Therefore, the recommendation of the ten men to Moses was not to attack the people in Canaan.

The other two men, Joshua and Caleb, told Moses that the Israelites should take possession of the land of Canaan, for they certainly could do it. (Note, God had told Moses He was giving the land of Canaan to the Israelites.)

What made ten of the men afraid and two unafraid? The answer is in what Joshua and Caleb told the whole Israelite assembly.

> The land we passed through and explored is exceedingly good. If the LORD is pleased with us, he will lead us into that land, a land flowing with milk and honey, and will give it to us. Only do not rebel against the LORD. And do not be afraid of the people of the land, because we will devour them. Their protection is gone, but the LORD is with us. Do not be afraid of them (Numbers 14:7–9 NIV).

It seems the ten men put their confidence in man, or themselves, while Joshua and Caleb put their confidence—or high expectations—in God.

So how were the lives of these twelve men affected? The ten men were struck down and died of a plague before the Lord. Joshua and Caleb were the only ones of the twelve to survive. All the other men, twenty years old and older, died as they wandered in the wilderness for forty years.

Another example that shows how expectations can affect lives is the story of David and Goliath.

The Israelites and the Philistines lined up for battle—one on one hill and the other on another hill—with a valley in between. Goliath, a Philistine champion, defied anyone from the Israelite camp to come and fight him. If the Israelite killed him, Goliath, the Philistines would become their subjects.

Goliath was described as being over nine feet tall. His armor weighed about 125 pounds, and the staff of his spear was like a weaver's beam with a head that weighed about fifteen pounds. His helmet and other armor were made of bronze.

All the Israelites, including their leader, Saul, were terrified of Goliath and the Philistines.

One day David's father told David to take some food to his brothers who were in the Israelite army. (David was the youngest child of his father's family and was a sheepherder.) He was at the battle line when Goliath came forward and shouted his defiance to the Israelites, as he had done for forty days. David also saw how the Israelites ran from Goliath with great fear. King Saul had offered great wealth, his daughter in marriage, and exemption from taxes to the man who would kill Goliath.

David volunteered to fight Goliath, but Saul told him he was not able to fight Goliath because he was only a boy and Goliath had been a fighting man from his youth. This is how David replied:

> Your servant has been keeping his father's sheep. When a lion or a bear came and carried off a sheep from the flock, I went after it, struck it and rescued the sheep from its mouth. When it turned on me, I seized it by its hair, struck it and killed it. Your servant has killed both the lion and the bear; this uncircumcised Philistine will be like one of them, because he has defied the armies of the living God. The LORD who

> rescued me from the paw of the lion and the paw of the bear will rescue me from the hand of this Philistine. Saul said to David, "Go, and the Lord be with you." (1 Samuel 17:34–37 NIV)

David refused to wear the usual battle dress but chose his staff, five smooth stones from a stream (which he put in his shepherd's bag), and his sling.

When David approached Goliath, the Philistine cursed David by his gods and told him that he would give his flesh to the birds of the air and the beasts of the field.

This did not scare David. He replied,

> You come against me with sword and spear and javelin, but I come against you in the name of the Lord Almighty, the God of the armies of Israel, whom you have defied. This day the Lord will deliver you into my hands, and I'll strike you down and cut off your head. This very day I will give the carcasses of the Philistine army to the birds and the wild animals, and the whole world will know that there is a God in Israel. All those gathered here will know that it is not by sword or spear that the Lord saves; for the battle is the Lord's, and he will give all of you into our hands. (1 Samuel 17:45–47 NIV)

As Goliath moved closer to David, David ran quickly toward him, slung a stone, and struck Goliath in the forehead and killed him. When the Philistines saw that David had killed Goliath, they ran with fear.

David showed King Saul he was not afraid, because he believed God would give him the strength to defeat Goliath. This story reminds me of what the apostle Paul told Timothy in 2 Timothy 1:7 "For God hath not given us the spirit of fear; but of power, and of love, and of a sound mind" (KJV).

Psalm 118—which some people believe David wrote—gives us some guidance to help boost our positive expectations (all verses are taken from the King James Version).

1. "O give thanks unto the Lord; for he is good: because his mercy endureth for ever" (v. 1).
2. "I called upon the LORD in distress: the LORD answered me, and set me in a large place" (v. 5).
3. "The LORD is on my side; I will not fear: what can man do unto me?" (v. 6).
4. "The LORD taketh my part with them that help me: therefore shall I see my desire upon them that hate me" (v. 7).
5. "It is better to trust in the LORD than to put confidence in man" (v. 8).
6. "It is better to trust in the LORD than to put confidence in princes" (v. 9).
7. "The LORD is my strength and song, and is become my salvation" (v. 14).
8. "I shall not die, but live, and declare the works of the LORD" (v. 17).
9. "The LORD hath chastened me sore: but he hath not given me over unto death" (v. 18).
10. "This is the LORD's doing; it is marvelous in our eyes" (v. 23).
11. "This is the day which the LORD hath made; we will rejoice and be glad in it" (v. 24).
12. "God is the LORD, which hath shewed us light: bind the sacrifice with cords, even unto the horns of the altar" (v. 27).
13. "Thou art my God, and I will praise thee: thou art my God, I will exalt thee" (v. 28).
14. "O give thanks unto the LORD; for he is good: for his mercy endureth for ever" (v. 29)

CHAPTER 2

Level of Expectation

Expectations Change

Since expectations are affected by experiences, knowledge, and circumstances, they may, or will, change as our experiences, knowledge, and circumstances change. For example, suppose you get into your car one morning—as you have for the last four years—to start the engine and it doesn't start right away, but it does start after you try many times. (Doesn't it appear that incidents like this occur when you are already late for the event you are going to?) After this experience, will you expect the car to start the next time like it did for the last four years ... or like it did the last time, or to not start at all? Either answer shows that your expectation for the car to start has changed. Because the car did not start quickly this time, doubt has entered your mind.

You go to work and tell your supervisor that you had a problem starting your car. Your supervisor may expect you to take some time off to get your car repaired, find another means of getting to work, have your car repaired after work, or be late getting to work. The change in your expectation of your car has now changed your supervisor's expectation of your car getting you to work on time.

When you take the car to a shop, you will expect the mechanic to correctly diagnose the problem. If he doesn't, your expectation of him will probably change.

Here is a personal example. While driving our nineteen-year-old car that my wife usually drives, I heard a noise that made me think something was wrong. Maybe something had been damaged when we drove the car through a couple of potholes. Since driving through potholes can damage a car's front-end alignment, I took the car to a local car dealer who had a special deal for four-wheel alignments. I described the noise to the service person when I requested the alignment. After their diagnosis, I was told they did not do the alignment because all four struts on the car needed replacement. The cost to replace the struts would have been approximately $1,800. I had not expected that cost. Instead of having that shop do the work, I took the car to an independent shop a friend had recommended to me. That shop said only the two rear struts needed replacement and charged me approximately $750. My expectations of the dealership's service department went down significantly; they went up significantly for the independent shop.

Just as your expectations change, your trust and faith in someone or something also change. Those changes can increase or decrease your faith and trust, depending on your attitude toward the focus of your expectations. In the example of the car-starting problem above, suppose the mechanic had found that your car needed a new battery. Your knowledge and experience with automobiles may have you focus on the battery after you conclude that the battery is expected to last about five years. Therefore, your trust in your car should not decrease much.

Even if there was no other recent problem with the car, your expectations of your car may remain low for a little while until you are comfortable again that the problem was definitely the battery. However, if the starting problem is just another of a number of problems you have been experiencing with the car, your trust may decrease significantly (especially if you have been looking for an excuse to get another car).

Impatience

I can't wait for you. What is taking you so long? Next time I will do it myself. Why doesn't that car get out of my way? I think most of us have said something similar to these statements, or we have had some people say them to us.

These types of statements indicate that events are not occurring as fast as we'd like. But have you noticed that most of the time hurrying does not help the situation much? Many times hurrying causes us to make choices we may regret later. Speeding in a car can lead to accidents, damage, someone being hurt, or a traffic ticket. Any of these results of speeding can lead to other problems. Still, most of us at some time rush more than we should. And if we think about the times the statements given at the beginning of this section occur, we may realize that many times they relate to our expectations of someone or something.

Patience is a virtue that all of us should strive for in our lives. Consider some things the Bible says about patience:

> But the fruit of the Spirit is love, joy, peace, forbearance [patience], kindness, goodness, faithfulness, gentleness and self-control. Against such things there is no law. (Galatians 5:22–23 NIV)

> And not only *that,* but we also glory in tribulations, knowing that tribulation produces perseverance [patience]; and perseverance [patience], character; and character, hope. Now hope does not disappoint, because the love of God has been poured out in our hearts by the Holy Spirit who was given to us. (Romans 5:3–5 NKJV)

> But thou, O man of God, flee these things; and follow after righteousness, godliness, faith, love, patience, meekness. (1 Timothy 6:11 KJV)

> Wherefore seeing we also are compassed about with so great a cloud of witnesses, let us lay aside every weight, and the sin which doth so easily beset us, and let us run with patience the race that is set before us, Looking unto Jesus the author and finisher of our faith; who for the joy that was set before him endured the cross, despising the shame, and is set down at the right hand of the throne of God. (Hebrews 12:1–2 KJV)

An impatient person does not allow sufficient time for his expectations to develop completely. "I want this or that, and I want it now" is a common statement or implied statement from an impatient person. "I have not gotten the answer I wanted to my prayer, so I will do something else" (implies God is not responding fast enough for that person). This attitude leads that person not to expect much or anything from God; or in other words, he does not trust God or cannot recognize God's response.

Also, the attitudes of an impatient person affect his relationships with others. What can others expect from an impatient person? Probably a short temper, a rush job (possibly an incomplete job), anger or an angry-sounding voice, intimidation, argument, etc.). In other words, you can expect an unhappy experience. The severity of these results depends on the severity of the impatience of the person.

So if you were asked if you trust an impatient person, what would you say? Hopefully by now you would say something like, I trust (expect) him to make a lot of comments about other drivers when he is driving. Or I expect him to give me an argument if he disagrees with me, and he will try to intimidate me to get me to agree with him. (Note that you expect him to perform at a particular level for a particular situation, as explained in chapter 1.)

Experience with Truck

Another example of a level of expectation is another experience with my truck. A man was helping me clean gutters on a building at my church. When we finished cleaning the gutters, he said another church official had asked him to pull up some bushes in front of the church. Seeing his smaller truck and the large bushes he had been asked to remove, I asked him if he wanted me to use my truck, since it was bigger and had four-wheel drive. He agreed to use my bigger truck, which we did.

The bushes were harder to pull up than I had thought. Each time we fastened the rope around some limbs near the bottom of a bush, the limbs would break off when we tried to pull the bush up. Finally, he shortened all the limbs and fastened the nylon rope around the "stump." With my truck in four-wheel drive, I had the truck move forward slowly and tighten the rope (bungee cord). Suddenly without any warning, the stump broke off abruptly with such force that the stump hit the tailgate on my truck and put two small dents in the tailgate. The damage occurred even though my truck was approximately five yards away from the stump. Fortunately, no one got hurt.

Later I wondered why the Lord had allowed that to happen to my truck, which was less than a year old. Here I was volunteering my time and truck to help beautify the church, and my truck got damaged. However, that was a learning experience for me.

What made me expect that just because I was doing something "good," I should expect God's favor? Job, in the Bible, was a righteous man, and he experienced more adverse things than I did—he experienced great physical pain, suffering, and loss.

That experience was a lesson for me to not think more highly of that truck than I ought to. For that reason I still have two dents on the tailgate of my truck and don't plan to have them repaired. They are a reminder of a lesson that happened many years ago.

"Follow Me"

I have noticed that there are three basic ways of controlling traffic when a bridge on a two-lane highway is being repaired or replaced.

A person with a sign that has "STOP" on one side and "SLOW" on the other side will communicate with another person at the other end of the construction who has a similar sign. One person stops the traffic on one end of the construction, while the other person at the other end lets the traffic through.

Another method is to have a traffic signal on each side of the construction.

The third method is to have a driver in a vehicle with a sign on the rear of the vehicle that reads, "FOLLOW ME." That sign begs a question, Have you ever seen anyone question the person in the vehicle to ask him or her where he or she was leading them? Probably the drivers in the vehicles that follow the vehicle with the sign have never seen the driver in that vehicle before that day. Seeing the bridge under construction may be enough for the drivers going through the construction area to expect the person in the truck to safely lead them around the construction area.

It amazes me to see how many people follow someone without fully understanding where their leader is taking them. They too must not require much evidence to expect their leader to lead them to their desired destination. Again, their expectations depend on their previous experiences and the present situation.

I am reminded of an incident that occurred many years ago. One of my coworkers had a son who piloted a plane with the Thunderbirds—the precision flying demonstration team for the Air Force. During one training session, four of the planes were flying in one of their formation maneuvers. While flying down toward the earth, the lead plane developed a malfunction in the control stick actuator, which meant the pilot could not control his plane. Because the other three pilots were cueing off the lead aircraft, and probably didn't know, or expect, that the lead plane had a problem, all four planes flew into the ground.

A lesson we can learn from this incident is, be careful whom we follow.

Seeing Is Believing?

Many people call the apostle Thomas "Doubting Thomas." In a way I give Thomas some credit. When the "disciples were together, with the doors locked for fear of the Jewish leaders, Jesus came and stood among them and said, 'Peace be with you!' After he said this, he showed them his hands and side. The disciples were overjoyed when they saw the Lord" (John 20:19–20 NIV).

> Now Thomas (also known as Didymus), one of the Twelve, was not with the disciples when Jesus came. So the other disciples told him, "We have seen the Lord!" But he said to them, "Unless I see the nail marks in his hands and put my finger where the nails were, and put my hand into his side, I will not believe." (John 20:24–25 NIV)

The apostle Thomas wanted creditable evidence before he believed the other disciples. Maybe people think Thomas was asking for too much evidence when he asked to put his finger where the nails were in Jesus and to put his hand into His side. Could it be that Thomas wanted more than seeing before he believed?

Herein lies something interesting. Most of us have heard the saying "Seeing is believing." However, once you see something that you believed in before you saw it, your belief, trust, faith, and expectation become a fact, in most cases. For example, if I had never seen you lift a one-hundred-pound weight, I could compare, in my mind, your stature, your muscles, and other characteristics with those of myself and someone else and determine if I think you could lift the weight. If I had some reservations that you could lift the weight, but thought there was a possibility that you could, then that could be an example of belief. If I were definitely sure, without seeing you lift any weight close to one hundred pounds, then that would be an example of faith. After I see you lift, or fail to lift, the weight, then I would know that you can or cannot lift the weight. Then there would be no need of belief, trust, faith, or expectation of your lifting that weight at that time and in your physical condition at that time.

Jesus Raised Lazarus

A high level of expectation was displayed by Mary and Martha in the biblical account of Jesus bringing Lazarus back to life after he had been dead for four days (see John 11:1–44). In separate instances both Mary and Martha told Jesus that if He had been there, their brother would not have died. They expected Jesus would have healed Lazarus if He had been there before their brother died. Martha further said, "But I know that even now God will give you whatever you ask" (v. 22 NIV).

However, based on what Martha said when Jesus said to take away the stone, I wonder if she still believed that Jesus could bring Lazarus back to life even after he had started to deteriorate. Martha said there would be a bad odor because Lazarus had been dead for four days. Jesus told Martha that if she believed—expected He could give Lazarus life again—she would see the glory of God. After that, the stone was removed from the grave, and Jesus prayed and called in a loud voice for Lazarus to come out, which he did.

Centurion's Servant

Another high level of expectation was shown by the centurion who came to Jesus on behalf of his servant, who was paralyzed and in great pain. When Jesus offered to go and heal the servant, the centurion objected. He said that he was not worthy of Jesus to come under his roof. However, because he had knowledge and experience as a commanding centurion soldier, he knew the power of a command. So with this understanding he believed that if Jesus said the word, his servant would be healed. Jesus complimented him by telling His followers that He had not found anyone in Israel with such great faith. He then told the centurion to go and it would be done as he, the centurion, believed it would. The servant was healed at that very time (see Matthew 5:8–13).

New Neighbors

Have you observed your expectations of a neighbor when a stranger moves next door into your neighborhood, housing complex, or workplace? Did past experiences with neighbors affect your expectations? Probably so! Were physical characteristics of the person or persons a factor? Probably so! What would make you be the first one to start a dialogue between you and your new neighbor?

The person who has had good experiences with neighbors may have higher expectations of a stranger than a person who has had not-so-good experiences with neighbors. A person who has had good and not-so-good experiences with previous neighbors may have low expectations of someone new because he realizes that a stranger may or may not come up to those expectations, thereby causing the person to be ashamed or hurt.

When a person starts with realistic expectations of a stranger, it allows both persons to build their faith in each other with minimal disappointments and hurt. Each neighbor should look for more positive aspects of his neighbor rather than negative ones, more likes than dislikes, and more encouragements than criticisms. There is a saying that goes something like this: You get what you look for (or expect).

Repair of Chair

Expectations of someone or something can be different for different people. For example, a neighbor put a broken wooden chair on the street for disposal. The chair had been used on an "open" deck of their house, so exposure to the weather had caused it to become weak in several places, and one part was even broken. To me, my neighbors' actions indicated that they did not expect the chair to fulfill the purpose of a chair.

When I looked at the chair on the street, I expected it would not take much for me to repair the chair and make it useful again. Since I did not know how sound/solid the wood was in the chair, my expectation had to be based on the appearance of the chair. It had one broken piece I thought I could easily fix.

When I started repairing the chair, I found other things wrong. At that point I could have, and maybe should have, put the chair back on the street for disposal. The chair was made of soft wood, so even after it was repaired the value would not be considered much. However, I kept repairing and replacing damaged parts.

The repair took longer than I had originally thought it would. I probably could have made a new one in the time it took me to make the repairs.

One day while I was repairing the chair, I asked myself why? Why was I putting so much time into repairing things like that chair? My answer was, I get enjoyment in taking something someone has thrown away, or think the item is no good, and turn it into something useful. Then the thought came to me, Isn't that what God does for us—take someone others consider no good and turn that person into someone beautiful and useful? We can expect that of God. And when we expect positive results from people and give them encouragement, we just may help them to become beautiful and useful.

"Bad" Person

What do you expect of a person who is known to be "bad"? How would you describe a "bad" person? Could he be a person who breaks or violates laws? Could he be one who continually breaks laws? Could he be a person who disrespects his parents or those in authority? Could he be a drug addict or substance abuse addict? Could he be a person who sexually abuses children? Could he be a person who does not accept Jesus Christ as his personal Savior? Could he be a person you think is being controlled by Satan?

To be more specific, would you say the following persons were "bad" people?

- Idi Amin Dada—killed 80,000 to 500,000 people in Uganda.
- Adolf Hitler—brought death and destruction to tens of millions of people.
- Josef Stalin—murdered 10 million to 60 million people.
- Osama bin Laden—founder of Al-Qaeda.
- Saddam Hussein—president of Iraq from 1979 to April 2003.
- Jim Jones—religious/cult leader who murdered or caused 909 of his members to commit suicide in Jonestown, Guyana.

Would you say the person in Mark 5:3–5 (NIV) was a "bad" person?

> This man lived in the tombs, and no one could bind him anymore, not even with a chain. For he had often been chained hand and foot, but he tore the chains apart and broke the irons on his feet. No one was strong enough to subdue him. Night and day among the tombs and in the hills he would cry out and cut himself with stones.

That is just part of the story of the man who lived in the tombs. Mark 5:1–2 (NIV) states, "They went across the lake to the region of the Gerasenes. When Jesus got out of the boat, a man with an impure spirit came from the tombs to meet him." Jesus commanded the unclean spirit to come out of the man.

Not only was there one unclean spirit in the man, there were many—enough to go into approximately two thousand nearby swine, which ran down a hill and drown in the sea. Afterward, the people who fed the swine and those in the city and country who heard about the incident asked Jesus to depart from their region. Did they think Jesus was "bad"?

The response I received from most Christians I asked to describe a "bad" person is that they believe there is no "bad" person, but people do bad things. I think when people say someone is "bad," they are describing someone who allows, or chooses to be influenced by, spiritual forces such as Satan, demons, or his sinful nature. However, keep in mind that some people who do good, but are different than others or think/believe differently than others, are considered to be "bad" by those who are different. For example, the Pharisees considered Jesus Christ to be "bad." The leaders of the Confederate army considered the leaders of the Yankees to be bad, and vice versa. Also, Robin Hood, an outlaw in English folklore, stole from the rich and gave to the poor; therefore, the rich would say that he was "bad," but the poor would say that he was good.

So what do you expect from a "bad" person? Are your expectations based on the person's physical features and actions, or are you looking beyond those? With help, some "bad" people can be encouraged to be good. Consider George Wallace, a strong segregationist governor of Alabama in the 1960s who did some mean things. He said that he became a Christian in the late 1970s, which led him to apologize to the people he had harmed when he was a segregationist.

The apostle Paul also made a drastic change in his life. Before the change in his life, he sought Christians to kill them. After his life changed, he spent his life helping people become Christians and educating them to live Christian lives. His writings comprise most of the New Testament in the Bible.

So when you begin to expect someone is "bad," remember that person is one of God's creations. If the person is different in some way from us, physically or ideologically, who is the "bad" person? Another thing to remember is that "but by the grace of God you or I could be that person."

The Unexpected and Levels of Faith

We have said much about expectations, but what about the unexpected? You probably have heard, or have said, I did not expect that to happen. Or, I did not expect him or her to be successful or to be worth anything.

What is the unexpected? It is something that is not expected, that is not seen or thought of beforehand, or that is surprising. The unexpected is not the same for everyone. Something may be unexpected by one person, whereas to another person it is expected.

So why does one person expect something to happen, while another person does not expect that same thing to happen? One possible explanation is different levels of faith. Remember the definition we gave earlier for faith in the introduction: a confident expectation that someone or something will perform to a particular level and having enough evidence to believe (or know) that what is expected has a possibility of happening.

There are many examples in the Bible to show how levels of faith affected the expectations of persons. Here are a few:

Jesus asked His disciples to get in a boat to go to the other side of a lake, while He remained to dismiss the crowd that He had miraculously fed. He wanted to be alone to pray. During the night or early morning (3:00–6:00 a.m.), Jesus went to the boat in an unexpected way—he was walking on the turbulent water of the lake (see Matthew 14:22–33).

The disciples were terrified to see something like a ghost coming toward them—Jesus was walking on the water. Immediately, Jesus identified Himself and told them to take courage and not be afraid.

At the request of the apostle Peter, Jesus invited him to come to Him on the water. Maybe without thinking, Peter also performed an unexpected event—he walked on the water toward Jesus until he saw that the wind was boisterous; then he began to sink.

Jesus saved him but told him that he had little faith and asked him, Why did you doubt?

Another example of how faith affects expectations also involves Jesus and His disciples. A man brought his son to the disciples to be healed (see Matthew 17:14–20). The son had seizures that caused him to often fall into fire and water, resulting in him suffering greatly. The man had brought his son to Jesus' disciples, but they could not heal the son.

After Jesus rebuked the demon and the demon came out of the boy, the disciples asked Jesus in private why they couldn't drive the demon out. Jesus told them that it was because they had so little faith. His reply also gives us the saying that if you have the faith of a mustard seed, you can move mountains.

There are other examples of people having little faith—such as when we worry about our lives, what we are going to eat or drink, or what we are going to wear (see Matthew 6:25–34).

Likewise, there is an example of great faith (see Matthew 8:5–13). As was previously mentioned, a centurion came to Jesus for help because his servant was paralyzed and was suffering terribly. Instead of the usual request for Jesus to go and heal the person, the centurion gave a different reply. He said that he did not deserve Jesus to come under his roof. He just wanted Jesus to say the word and his servant would be healed. His reply astonished Jesus, and He said to those following Him that He had not found anyone in Israel with such great faith.

So from these examples of little and great faith, it seems we can conclude that little expectations give little faith and great expectations yield great faith. This short or concise summary of expectations and faith can be explained by using the definition of faith derived earlier.

That definition of faith is "a confident expectation that someone or something will perform to a particular level and having enough evidence to believe (or know) that what is expected has a possibility of happening." This could be the definition of little faith. For great faith the definition could be revised to read, "*Great* faith is an *unquestionably* confident expectation that someone or something will perform to a particular level and having enough evidence to support a good basis for believing (or knowing) that what is expected has an *excellent* possibility of happening."

There is an example in the Bible that I think shows the unexpected, little faith, and great faith. Acts 3:1–8 describes how the apostles Peter and John helped a crippled man. The man, who had been crippled from birth, was carried to the temple gate every day to beg from those entering the temple. When he saw Peter and John entering the temple, he asked them for money. Peter and John looked straight at him, and Peter said, "Look at us!" So the man gave them his attention, expecting to get something from them. "Then Peter said, 'Silver or gold I do not have, but what I do have I give you. In the name of Jesus Christ of Nazareth, walk'" (Acts 3:4–7, NIV). Peter helped the man up, and instantly the man's feet and ankles became strong.

In this example it seems the man demonstrated little faith. When he saw Peter and John, he expected them to give him money. At first he expected money, but when Peter told him to look at them, what happened next as described above was totally different from what the man had originally requested. Considering who Peter and John were, the question is, did he have enough evidence to expect much more?

Even though Peter had demonstrated little faith when he went to meet Jesus on the water, as described above, he and John seem to have had great faith in this latter case. They seemed to have unquestioning expectations that the man would be healed and they expected there was an excellent possibility that the healing would occur. What Peter and John did was expected by the two of them but was apparently unexpected by the crippled man.

Yet Peter tells us in chapter 4 of Acts that it was not what he and John did that healed the man. He let it be known that the man was healed by the name of Jesus Christ of Nazareth.

And so it is with most, if not all, of our levels of expectations. It is not so much what we do that gives us our levels of expectations, but in many cases these levels depend on our level of faith in God.

CHAPTER 3

God

What Do You Expect from God?

- Do you trust God? What do you expect from Him?
- Do you expect Him to give you everything you ask for, through prayer, in faith?
- Do you expect Him to physically heal your loved one when you pray for healing?
- Do you expect Him to provide rain when you ask for it and sunshine when you ask for it too?
- Do you expect Him to give you comfort and joy, and other special privileges because you are one of His followers?
- Do you expect Him to allow you to win the $100 million lottery because you would give Him His tithe or you would give a lot to charitable organizations?
- Do you expect Him to provide all your needs and many of your wants?
- Do you expect Him to give you what you ask for if it is in accordance with His will, His purpose, and His timing?
- Do you expect God to say yes to some of the things you ask for, say no to some things, and say wait to other things? Do you have this expectation because you believe He has something

better for you or that He knows that what you are asking for will be harmful for you?

- Do you expect Him to keep His Word?

These questions are presented to stimulate your thoughts of what you may expect from God. Do you think your answers today are the same as your answers would have been five or ten years ago? If you have grown in knowledge, experiences, and wisdom of God during those times, some of your answers may be different. That is because your growth in knowledge, experiences, and wisdom of God probably increased (or should have increased) your faith and trust in Him.

Remember the discussion of trust in chapter 1—a confident expectation that someone or something will perform at a particular level for a particular situation. As your trust in God increases, you will begin to realize that He will not do anything that is outside His will. For example, if you ask God for something that would result in your breaking one of His commandments, He will not grant you that request. Or suppose you ask the Lord not to let your dad and mom die each time they get sick. That means you expect God to have them live on this earth forever in their present physical bodies.

Trusting God with all your heart requires you to study His Word so you will learn His will and thereby establish a correct level for your expectations. Someone has said, never measure God's unlimited power by your limited expectations.

Now let's change the one who is expecting. What do you think God expects from you? I can give you a few things He said in His Word.

In the Old Testament people thought they should bow down before God, offer sacrifices, and do similar things. But He tells us the following in Micah 6:6–8 (NKJV):

> With what shall I come before the Lord, And bow myself before the High God? Shall I come before Him with burnt offerings, With calves a year old? Will the Lord be pleased with thousands of rams, Ten thousand rivers

> of oil? Shall I give my firstborn for my transgression, The fruit of my body for the sin of my soul? He has shown you, O man, what is good; And what does the LORD require of you But to do justly, To love mercy, And to walk humbly with your God?

Note the last statement. God wants us to act justly, to love mercy, and to walk humbly with Him.

In the New Testament Jesus answered a question a lawyer asked Him, who was tempting Him, about the greatest commandment (Matthew 22:37–40 KJV).

> Jesus said unto him, Thou shalt love the Lord thy God with all thy heart, and with all thy soul, and with all thy mind. This is the first and great commandment. And the second is like unto it, Thou shalt love thy neighbour as thyself. On these two commandments hang all the law and the prophets.

God expects us to love Him better than we love anyone or anything else. Also, we should love our neighbor as we love ourselves.

There are many expectations of God in the New Testament. All of them are meant for our good. He does not want anyone to perish but everyone to come to repentance (see 2 Peter 3:9).

We can trust God. We can expect Him to perform to the level of His will at any time. He is faithful. His wisdom is beyond our understanding. His ways are not our ways. He knows the future. His love for us far exceeds our expectations and understanding. Consider what the apostle Paul says in Ephesians 3:20–21 (NKJV): "Now to Him who is able to do exceedingly abundantly above all that we ask or think, according to the power that works in us, to Him be glory in the church by Christ Jesus to all generations, forever and ever. Amen."

What Do You Expect from the Holy Spirit?

You have probably heard Christians use the following scripture passages to encourage, inspire, and inform others, or to inspire themselves:

> So the Lord said, "If you have faith as a mustard seed, you can say to this mulberry tree, 'Be pulled up by the roots and be planted in the sea,' and it would obey you." (Luke 17:6 NKJV)

> I can do all things through Christ who strengthens me. (Philippians 4:13 NKJV)

> You are of God, little children, and have overcome them, because He who is in you is greater than he who is in the world. (1 John 4:4 NKJV)

What should a Christian expect when he receives or gives scriptures like these? After hearing a sermon based on 1 John 4:4 and during a discussion on "greater is He who is in you than he who is in the world," this thought came to me—*He who is in you is only as strong as you let Him.*

Let me explain. For Christians, He who is in you is the Holy Spirit (see note 1, chapter 1). Likewise, he who is in the world refers to Satan, the prince of this world. God controls Satan; therefore He is much more powerful than Satan. According to what the apostle Paul says in Ephesians 3:20 (NIV), "Now to him who is able to do immeasurably more than all we ask or imagine, according to his power that is at work within us." The power that works within us is the Holy Spirit; therefore, He can do immeasurably more than all we ask or imagine. Think of that—He can do immeasurably more than we can ask or imagine. That is power.

So when I say the Holy Spirit is only as strong as you let Him be, I am not saying that you can control the power of the Holy Spirit, but you can influence the amount of power the Holy Spirit can manifest through you.

For example, a Christian may need to use self-examination to determine if He who is in him (the Christian) is greater than he who is in the world. A Christian who reads and studies his Bible daily, who has godly and positive attitudes and motives for during things, who puts God first in all things, who trusts in the Lord with all his heart, who loves the Lord with all his mind, soul, and body and his neighbor as himself, etc., may expect better results than a Christian who does the opposite. (Note: he may expect better results based on God's perspective rather than on a human perspective.)

A Christian needs to use the Bible as a basis for self-examination. For example, the apostle Paul gives us information in the book of Galatians that is helpful in self-examination (Galatians 5:16–26 NIV).

> So I say, live by the Spirit, and you will not gratify the desires of the sinful nature. For the sinful nature desires what is contrary to the Spirit, and the Spirit what is contrary to the sinful nature. They are in conflict with each other, so that you do not do what you want. But if you are led by the Spirit, you are not under law.
>
> The acts of the sinful nature are obvious: sexual immorality, impurity and debauchery; idolatry and witchcraft; hatred, discord, jealousy, fits of rage, selfish ambition, dissensions, factions and envy; drunkenness, orgies, and the like. I warn you, as I did before, that those who live like this will not inherit the kingdom of God.
>
> But the fruit of the Spirit is love, joy, peace, patience, kindness, goodness, faithfulness, gentleness and self-control. Against such things there is no law. Those who belong to Christ Jesus have crucified the sinful nature with its passions and desires. Since we live by the Spirit, let us keep in step with the Spirit. Let us not become conceited, provoking and envying each other.

After the self-examination, the Christian should answer this question: Am I letting He who is in me be greater than he who is trying to tempt me to do wrong and to steal, kill, or destroy me? Your answer affects your expectations from the Holy Spirit.

God Can Exceed Expectations When There Is a Need

Once when Jesus was on a mountainside with his disciples, He ministered to a great crowd. The crowd was large, and they were in a remote area. As evening approached, the disciples suggested that they send the crowd away so the crowd could go to the villages and buy themselves some food. Jesus told the disciples that the crowd didn't have to go away. He asked the disciples to feed them. Jesus asked Philip, one of His disciples, where they could buy bread for the people. Philip said that eight months' wages could not buy enough cheap bread for each person to have one bite.

Andrew, another disciple of Jesus, said that a lad had five barley loaves and two small fishes but asked how far that could go in feeding the crowd.

Jesus and the disciples saw a need—the crowd needed something to eat. Also, Jesus saw a need to test Philip. However, Jesus knew how He was going to feed the crowd, but the disciples expected the crowd to get their own food, since they, the disciples, did not have enough food to feed all of them.

Jesus took the loaves of bread and the fish, blessed and broke them, and gave them to the disciples for distribution to the crowd. After the people had had enough to eat, the disciples gathered twelve baskets full of the pieces that were left over. There were about five thousand men—not counting the women and children (see Matthew 14:15–21 and John 6:5–13).

Do you expect this incident happened as explained in the Bible? Or do you have or look for a *practical* explanation? If you were one of the disciples, would you have expected Jesus to feed the crowd with two fish and five loaves of bread? If you were the lad, would you have freely given your lunch? When you have an *impossible* situation, what do you expect from God? If someone has an *impossible* situation, will you freely give to God one of your prized possession for Him to use, like the lad did? Abraham was willing to sacrifice his son as described in Genesis 22 (NKJV).

> Now it came to pass after these things that God tested Abraham, and said to him, "Abraham!" And he said, "Here I am." Then He said, Take now your son, your only son Isaac, whom you love, and go to the land of Moriah, and offer him there as a burnt offering on one of the mountains of which I shall tell you (vv. 1–2).

> But the Angel of the Lord called to him from heaven and said, "Abraham, Abraham!" So he said, "Here I am." And He said, "Do not lay your hand on the lad, or do anything to him; for now I know that you fear God, since you have not withheld your son, your only son, from Me" (vv. 11–12).

> Then the Angel of the Lord called to Abraham a second time out of heaven, and said: "By Myself I have sworn, says the Lord, because you have done this thing, and have not withheld your son, your only son—blessing I will bless you, and multiplying I will multiply your descendants as the stars of the heaven and as the sand which is on the seashore; and your descendants shall possess the gate of their enemies. In your seed all the nations of the earth shall be blessed, because you have obeyed My voice (vv. 15–18).

Fear Affects Expectations.

As I grow in knowledge of the Bible and observe my actions and those of others, I am amazed how much fear influences our lives.

That influence can be positive or negative, because to me fear can be considered good or bad.

Fear can be considered good when it can prevent you from experiencing harm or reduce the severity of the harm, physically or spiritually.

When I was young, I was afraid to walk under a ladder because people said it would bring me bad luck. (Note, as I am a Christian, *luck* should have no bearing on my life, because God is sovereign.) No matter how I grew spiritually, it bothered me to walk under a ladder. One day after dropping something while I was working on a ladder, it occurred to me that the statement about walking under a ladder had a valid meaning. If I and the person working on the ladder were not careful, something could fall on me from the ladder and hurt me. Therefore, the fear of walking under a ladder can be a good fear.

Likewise, the fear of high places, the fear of snakes, the fear of bears, the fear of riding a bicycle on a busy street, and the fear of jumping into deep water (if you don't know how to swim) are all good fears provided they are not obsessive or irrational. I am calling the obsessive and irrational fears "bad" for the lack of better words.

Another good fear is reverent fear; for example, fear of God and parents. This type of fear results from a deep respect for God and parents. When parents discipline their children in love and with consistency, a parent can communicate disapproval to the child without saying a word. The parent can look at a child a certain way, and the child will know that he or she must be doing something that the parent does not approve of.

In a way, reverent fear is difficult to explain. Even though the child may fear that the parent may apply some form of discipline, the child does not go through with his or her actions, because it may also hurt the parent—emotionally or mentally. Or sometimes it may be a combination of both hurts.

Reverent fear of God is similar. God is all-powerful, and His love for us is not a selfish love. He disciplines us so that our relationship with

Him will improve—it is for our good. He tells us in 1 John 4:18 (NIV), "There is no fear in love. But perfect love drives out fear, because fear has to do with punishment. The one who fears is not made perfect in love." This love is so unique that as it grows, it can get to the point that the reverent fear becomes similar to no fear as in perfect love. Perfect love is the agape-type love.

However, a person can have no fear of God and also no love for Him. This is another reason why it is difficult for me to explain reverent fear.

When people do not fear God and/or love Him and His Word, what do they use to determine what is right and wrong? What do they use as a basis for their morals? If governments do not use the principles of the Bible to develop and interpret their laws, what should they use? What should be the basis for law and order? What should we expect from those in authority over us if they use some other source?

When a Christian has reverent fear of God, you should expect him to show love, joy, peace, patience, kindness, goodness, faithfulness, gentleness, and self-control. These are fruit of the Spirit (see Galatians 5:22–23).

From my observations, in general, we may expect some of the following reactions to fear:

- When a person fears criticism, we may expect him to lie.
- When a person fears he will bring shame and embarrassment to those who love him, we may expect him to lie, give excuses, and blame others.
- When a person is fearful of being hurt physically or mentally, we may expect him to lie, accuse others, and give excuses. An example of this fear in the Bible is that of the apostle Peter when Jesus was before the high priest. Jesus had told Peter earlier—before He was taken before the high priest—that he, Peter, would deny Him three times before the cock crowed. This was the outcome:

> And when they had kindled a fire in the midst of the hall, and were set down together, Peter sat down among them. But a certain maid beheld him as he sat by the fire, and earnestly looked upon him, and said, This man was also with him. And he denied him, saying, Woman, I know him not. And after a little while another saw him, and said, Thou art also of them. And Peter said, Man, I am not. And about the space of one hour after another confidently affirmed, saying, Of a truth this fellow also was with him: for he is a Galilaean. And Peter said, Man, I know not what thou sayest. And immediately, while he yet spake, the cock crew. And the Lord turned, and looked upon Peter. And Peter remembered the word of the Lord, how he had said unto him, Before the cock crow, thou shalt deny me thrice. And Peter went out, and wept bitterly. (Luke 22:55–62 KJV)

- When a person is afraid of being hurt or killed, we may expect him to defend himself.
- When a person is greedy for money and power and is afraid he does not have enough, we may expect him to lie, cheat, and do what he thinks necessary to gain more money and power.
- When Christians go to a public place to eat and are fearful of what people may say, you may expect some of them to not bless their food, or to bless it in an unnoticeable way.

But fear does not always produce the general expectations given above, as some of us know.

There is the example of a high school girl who was confronted by a gunman who asked if she was a Christian. I can imagine she was expecting the gunman to kill her if she said yes, but she said yes anyway and was killed.

The Bible says there was a woman who had had a bleeding condition for twelve years. Instead of getting better, she was getting worse even though she had seen many doctors. When she touched Jesus' clothes while He was in a crowd and received healing, He asked who had touched His clothes. She fell at His feet and, trembling with fear, told Him the whole truth (see Luke 8:43–48).

However, there are many examples in the Bible that support the general expectations above. For example, the Bible also gives the account of a man and wife who sold some of their property and kept some of the money for themselves; but they indicated to the apostle Peter that they were giving it all to the church. Peter told them that they had lied to the Holy Spirit. Their lies cause both of them to die. This incident changed the expectations of many people, because the whole church was seized with fear (see Acts 5:1–10).

So what makes people react/expect differently to fear? Consider the definition given earlier for trust—expecting someone or something to perform at a particular level for a particular situation. If a person faces a situation where he expects someone to hurt him, physically or mentally, he may quickly evaluate his options. If he thinks telling the truth will give him better results, he will tell the truth. But if he thinks lying will give better results, he will lie. That may be why some people will say, If I knew then what I know now, I would have made a different decision.

Then it seems our decisions are based on whom or what we trust the most. For example, a child takes a cookie when he thinks no one sees him doing it. His mother comes to him later and says, Did you take a cookie? The child may quickly evaluate his situation. If he thinks his discipline will be harsh—to him it is harsh—for taking the cookie and he expects there is no convicting evidence against him, he may lie and say he did not take the cookie. He trusts his stealing skills more than his mom's surveillance and investigative skills. But if he is about to tell a lie and sees a cookie crumb on his shirt, he may tell the truth. All of a sudden he realizes his stealing skills are not good, because the evidence is in plain sight. Or if from past experiences he expects his mom already knows the answer, he may tell the truth to keep from getting into greater trouble.

Adults react to similar situations in similar ways. Even though adults may—or should—have more knowledge and experience, the procedure for deciding whom or what to trust the most is similar. For Christians, the level of trust in God becomes a contributing factor. Do they trust themselves more than they trust God? In other words, do they expect God to guide them out of their situation, or do they expect themselves to do what they think needs to be done? Therefore, Christians may ask themselves questions like these: What would God want me to do? What does the Bible say I should do? What would other Christians think of me? Would it hurt my Christian testimony? The more they trust God, the greater influence He will have on their decisions and expectations. Perfect love drives out fear.

Also, in 2 Timothy 1:7 (KJV), the Bible says, "For God hath not given us the spirit of fear; but of power, and of love, and of a sound mind."

Positive Expectations Can Overshadow Doubts.

When your problems seem to weigh you down; when the problems linger without resolutions; and when you think God is not listening, what do you do? What are your expectations?

Do you turn against everyone, including God? Do you feel no one wants to help you, so you do not expect anything from anybody? Do you become bitter, angry, antisocial, lonely, and a person whom most people will choose not to associate with?

Or do you try to show that nothing is wrong, with smiles, pleasant expressions, and other actions you think a Christian should show? If you do, you are giving a false impression that your life is "sunny" when it is not. Hiding your problems could be making your life more miserable. Some people may think that by ignoring problems, the problems may go away. In some situations that may be true, but what happens when the problems do not go away? So it seems the best approach is to ask God to help you find solutions to your problems and have a positive expectation that He will.

In Psalm 13 King David seemed to have faced his problems head-on—at least at one time. In this psalm he seemed to have been a little discouraged at first and may have thought God had forgotten him and his enemies were triumphing over him. Later in the psalm he thought about the goodness and sovereignty of the Lord and said, I trust in your unfailing love, God, and my heart rejoices in your salvation.

That leads me to believe that our reactions to problems may show our spiritual foundation. Consider what Paul said in 1 Corinthians 3:10–15. He used gold, silver, precious stones, wood, hay, and stubble to describe the foundation of man's work. He said, "Every man's work shall be made manifest: for the day shall declare it, because it shall be revealed by fire; and the fire shall try every man's work of what sort it is" (v. 13 KJV).

If you put gold, silver, precious stones, wood, hay, and stubble (stumps remaining from crops that have been cut) into a fire, what would remain? If you said the first three, you are correct—the last three would burn up. The apostle Paul says the first three items represent a foundation based upon the Lord Jesus Christ.

Basing our foundation on Jesus helps us to have more positive expectations. Let's use Psalm 6 to show how David changed his view of his situation by changing his focus from himself to God.

In the first part of this psalm, David explained his condition:

- He was faint (v. 2).
- His bones were in agony (v. 2).
- His soul was in anguish (v. 3).
- He needed deliverance (v. 4).
- He was worn out from groaning (v. 6).
- He flooded his bed with tears all night long (v. 6).
- He drenched his couch with tears (v. 6).
- His eyes grew weaker with sorrow (v. 7).

In the last three verses David must have turned his focus from his problems and put his focus on God, because he started describing what the Lord had done for him:

- The Lord had heard the voice of his weeping (v. 8).
- The Lord had heard his supplication (v. 9).
- The Lord would receive his prayer (v. 9).

David went from an *oh, pity me* condition to a positive condition with high expectations of the Lord.

This is sound advice for someone who is worrying about a problem. That person should pray about the situation, turn it over to God, and from that time forward put his focus on God rather than on his problem. He should think about how God could solve his problem, and he should think about how God had brought him through problems before. He should read and study his Bible. But he shouldn't think about how he could solve the problem himself.

We can use a practical example to show the importance of having a correct focus. When a photographer takes a picture, he must make sure the camera is focused on the object that will be important in the photograph. If he focuses on something that is not at the same distance as the object of importance, the object will be fuzzy on the photograph.

Therefore, focus by itself is not as important as the object of the focus. As long as the apostle Peter had his focus on Jesus, he was able to defy gravity and walk on water. When he changed his focus to the wind and the surrounding conditions, he became afraid and started to sink. When a photographer focuses the camera on a distant object rather than on the object he wants to be clear in the photograph, the finished photograph is undesirable. Likewise, when a person puts his focus more on a problem than on the solution of the problem, God, the results can be—among other things—frustrating, stressful, and hurtful.

There was a time when I would take pictures of two people beside each other, using an automatic focusing camera, I would put the "area of focus" in the viewfinder between the two people I was photographing. I was doing this to make sure both people were centered on the resulting photograph. It took me a long time to determine why the people were not in focus on the photograph. I even thought something was wrong with the camera. One day the answer came to me. The people were not in focus on the photograph, because I did not put the "area of focus" in the camera on the people. Therefore, the camera was focusing on whatever was in the space between the people. Isn't that like us at times? We think we are focusing on God, when in reality we are focusing on something else.

Visible and Invisible

Hebrews 11:1 (KJV) says, "Now faith is the substance of things hoped for, the evidence of things not seen." What evidence do you have, or need, for you to have faith in God? You need evidence because God is invisible—you cannot see Him.

This need became more evident to me while I was listening to a discussion on Colossians 1:15 in a Bible study session. During that time, a thought came to me that showed why we need faith/expectations to serve God. Colossians 1:15a (NIV) states, "The Son [Jesus] is the image of the invisible God."

To provide us with the evidence stated in Hebrews 11:1, God sent His Son in the visible form of man. The apostle Paul says in Colossians 1:15 that Jesus is the image, an exact representation, of God. In John 10:30, Jesus says He and His Father are one, not two identical persons but are one in terms of both nature and essence.

When Philip asked Jesus to show them (the apostles) the Father, Jesus replied,

> Don't you know me, Philip, even after I have been among you such a long time? Anyone who has seen me has seen the Father. How can you say, 'Show us the Father'? Don't you believe that I am in the Father, and

> that the Father is in me? The words I say to you I do not speak on my own authority. Rather, it is the Father, living in me, who is doing his work. Believe me when I say that I am in the Father and the Father is in me; or at least believe on the evidence of the works themselves. (John 14:9–11 NIV)

The evidence was given differently in the Old Testament of the Bible when God spoke directly to some people, even though they didn't see His face. Those people then passed that information on to others. Since Jesus came, God can speak to us through His Word, the Holy Spirit, and others who respond to His commands, guidance, instructions, and so forth.

Another way of looking at the need for evidence to understand the invisible is to consider your trying to find out what another person is thinking, or what you expect the person is thinking. You may have heard, or said yourself, I know what you are thinking. But do you? A person's thoughts are invisible. The more evidence you have of what that person is thinking, the closer you may come to stating what the person is thinking. The longer you are around the person and share intimate thoughts, the better you can guess what the person may be thinking.

Good and proper evidence is important in choosing Christianity or any other religion, especially those that do not have "living" (in the physical form) leaders. For example, in choosing your religion, didn't your expectations of that religion rely on the evidence you had on the leader of that religion or on the doctrine of that leader? (Note: I am not referring to denominations.) You may not have given much thought to your choice of religion if you were raised by your loved ones in that religion. Some people may say, If it was good enough for my mother and father, it must be good enough for me. Even if the religion may not be all you would like for it to be, you may not want to challenge it, because the results may encourage a change—such as a change in your lifestyle, a change in the way you view your parents' values (maybe your basic values), or a change in your relationships.

I imagine most of us Christians have not had to decide which religion to accept. However, if you have, or if you do, think about what Joshua told the children of Israel:

> Now therefore, fear the LORD, serve Him in sincerity and in truth, and put away the gods which your fathers served on the other side of the River and in Egypt. Serve the LORD! And if it seems evil to you to serve the LORD, choose for yourselves this day whom you will serve, whether the gods which your fathers served that were on the other side of the River, or the gods of the Amorites, in whose land you dwell. But as for me and my house, we will serve the LORD. (Joshua 24:14–15 NKJV)

While I was studying a Sunday school lesson on God's mercy in the book of Micah, a unique characteristic of God was revealed to me. Micah 7:18a (NKJV) says, "Who is a God like You, Pardoning iniquity And passing over the transgression of the remnant of His heritage?" In other words, can other gods pardon sins and forgive transgressions like the heavenly Father? Christians can expect their invisible God to do those things.

Examples of Expectations in the Bible

Many verses in the Bible tell us what to expect from actions we take. Consider the first twelve verses in the third chapter of Proverbs (NIV):

1. Action—"[D]o not forget my [God's] teaching, but keep my commands in your heart" (v. 1).
   Expectation—"[T]hey will prolong your life many years and bring you peace and prosperity" (v. 2).

2. Action—"Let love and faithfulness never leave you; bind them around your neck, write them on the tablet of your heart" (v. 3).
   Expectation—"[Y]ou will win favor and a good name in the sight of God and man" (v. 4).

3. Action—"Trust in the LORD with all your heart and lean not on your own understanding; in all your ways submit to him" (vv. 5 and 6).
   Expectation—"He will make your paths straight" (v. 6).

4. Action—"Do not be wise in your own eyes; fear the LORD and shun evil" (v. 7).
   Expectation—"This will bring health to your body and nourishment to your bones" (v. 8).

5. Action—"Honor the LORD with your wealth, with the first fruits of all your crops" (v. 9).
   Expectation -[Y]our barns will be filled to overflowing, and your vats will brim over with new wine" (v. 10).

6. Action—"[D]o not despise the LORD's discipline, and do not resent his rebuke" (v. 11).
   Expectation - "[T]he LORD disciplines those he loves, as a father the son he delights in" (v. 11).

Consider another proverb that many Christians can recite, Proverbs 22:6 (KJV):

> Action—"Train up a child in the way he should go."
>
> Expectation—"When he is old, he will not depart from it."

CHAPTER 4

Prayer

Expectation in Prayer

Another way of describing faith is *acting* like your expectations will occur or are real to you. These expectations of yours are for someone or something to perform at a particular level for a particular situation.

So when you pray, do you expect God to perform to your expected level or do you expect God to perform to His level for you? For example, you need transportation to get to work, so you ask God for a car. Since you go to church every Sunday and pay your tithes, you may expect God to give you, or allow you to get, a late-model car. That is your level of expectation.

However, God may give you a ten-year-old car that is in good shape, looks good, and runs well. That may be God's level for you. Note, this is not saying that this is the best that God could do for you at that particular time. This is saying that God is giving you what He knows is best for you at that time. Even though you may not realize it, God knows that if He gave you a late-model car, you would be going somewhere else other than church, washing your car rather than going to church or helping others, or not offering someone a ride because you think he may mess up your nice car. So He gives you a car that will help you maintain, or improve, your Christian walk.

Instead of a car, God may give you another means of getting to church and to work. Or He may give you something other than a car, something that would require you to be responsible. If He gives you something other than a car, He may be showing you that you are not ready for the responsibility of a car. You may not recognize that, so you may think God did not answer your prayer. However, He did answer your prayer but not in the way you expected Him to answer it.

Many Christians tell you that God can answer your prayers in one of three ways: yes, no, and wait. However, God has revealed to me that there is another answer to consider. As discussed in the situation above, God may respond in a way different than the way you expect. So when it seems as though you have not received an answer to your prayer, look for other ways that He could have answered it. Therefore, God can answer our prayers in one of four ways: yes, no, wait, and I am giving you something better than what you asked for.

I have experienced that fourth answer. When I was in college, I asked God to help me get a good grade on a test. You may be thinking that I had been partying and wanted God to compensate for my lack of studying. However, I had studied. I also said at the end of my prayer what I had been taught to say—not my will but your will, Lord.

When I got my test results back, I got a grade lower than I had expected. So had God answered my prayer in one of the ways yes, no, or wait? At the time I did not know what to think, which led me to wonder about my spiritual standing with God.

Sometime after receiving that grade, while I was studying the Bible, I realized that God gave me an answer better than the good grade I had asked for and expected. He showed me that I did not mean what I said in my prayer. My reaction to the lower grade showed that I wanted God to satisfy my will—not His will for me.

Communication with God, prayer, is more than saying learned phrases or statements. Talking with God should be similar to talking with a loving parent. If you consider prayer in that manner, you may not be like some Christians who are afraid to pray in a group setting because they are concerned about what people may say about their choice of words. I know, because at one time I was terrified to pray in a group setting. I think God is more concerned about our sincerity, attitude, and love for Him than for our choice of words. Sometimes I am touched more in a group setting by a *simple* prayer of a child than I am by the *eloquent* prayer of an adult.

Expectations from Prayer

What do you expect when you pray? Since prayer is communication with God, you should expect God to hear your prayer. If you don't expect Him to hear your prayer, then there would be no need for you to pray. Even babies cry out to someone greater than themselves when they have a need. And when loving parents hear their child's cry, they respond to satisfy that need. So it is with sincere prayer to God.

Jesus says in Matthew 7:7–8 (NIV), "Ask and it will be given to you; seek and you will find; knock and the door will be opened to you. For everyone who asks receives; the one who seeks finds; and to the one who knocks, the door will be opened."

So when you pray, how do you expect God to answer your prayer? For example, do you expect Him to give you exactly what you ask for, and in accordance with your timetable? Generally, His answer can be in one of four ways, as described in the previous section. Let's expand those four ways. He may respond by giving you what you asked for. Or He may respond by saying, "No, I will not give you what you have asked for." Or He may respond by saying you must wait. Or He may respond by giving you something different than what you asked for but that is better for you.

An answer other than yes seems to challenge the faith of some people. This reaction may occur because God's answer, other than yes, is not as simple as I have stated in the last paragraph. Even a yes answer may be a challenge.

How can a yes answer be a challenge? Because God may not give you exactly what you asked for but He may give you what is best for you. So when you don't get what you exactly asked for, don't doubt God, but look to see if He may have given you something else. Refer to my example in the last section, when I didn't get the grade on an examination that I had prayed for and expected.

Another personal example can show how God could give you something that may be different from what you may expect. One Christmas when my two children were in their late teens or early twenties, I gave one some toilet tissue and the other some paper towels. I did this to see if they appreciated whatever gift we gave them. They were disappointed with their gifts even though they were useful gifts. They did not know or expect that I had placed money inside the gifts. We can be like my children—God may give us something less than what we ask for so that we may evaluate ourselves, especially our attitudes, worthiness, pride, selfishness, and other qualities. Being appreciative of what God gives us can help us improve our relationship with Him.

Consider the great apostle Paul, the writer of many books in the New Testament in the Bible. Three times he pleaded with the Lord to take away the thorn that was in his flesh. (Many Bible scholars believe the thorn was a severe affliction, not a physical thorn from a bush or tree.) The Lord's response to Paul's plea was, "My grace is sufficient for you, for my power is made perfect in weakness" (2 Corinthians 12:9 NIV). Paul did not get what he prayed for and expected, but he appreciated the more important results ... it kept him humble.

The Bible gives us another good example of a person getting something in a way that he did not expect. Naaman was a commander of an army and a highly regarded valiant soldier, but he had leprosy. Fortunately, his wife had a young slave girl who knew a prophet that could heal Naaman of his leprosy. A more detailed description of this example is given in chapter 6 of this book.

Not getting what we ask for from God is sometimes difficult for many Christians. Some people may start asking themselves and others why. Why doesn't God answer their prayer? They tithe, they go to church regularly, and they do other "good" things a Christian should do. They may even compare themselves with other Christians who do not do as much "for the Lord." Or they may compare themselves with people who are not Christians and who are getting more and better material things than they are.

When some people don't get what they ask for, they may even question God. They may say God should know what they need, so why doesn't He give them what they ask for? Also, God says that He provides for all our needs. They may refer to Matthew 7:9–11, where Jesus says that if you ask, it will be given to you. Additionally, He says that if a father knows how to give good gifts to his children, how much more will our heavenly Father give good gifts to those who ask?

In response to those questions, God could ask those people questions like He asked Job in the book of Job (NIV): Some of those questions are:

- "Where were you when I laid the earth's foundation? Tell me, if you understand" (Job 38:4).
- "Have you ever given orders to the morning, or shown the dawn its place, that it might take the earth by the edges and shake the wicked out of it?" (Job 38:12–13).
- "Can you raise your voice to the clouds and cover yourself with a flood of water? Do you send the lightning bolts on their way? Do they report to you, 'Here we are'?" (Job 38:34–35).
- "Do you know when the mountain goats give birth? Do you watch when the doe bears her fawn?" (Job 39:1).

God's questions could help us consider who we are to question His decisions. He is sovereign. Then we should remember what He said in Isaiah 55:8–9 (NIV): "For my thoughts are not your thoughts, neither are your ways my ways, declares the Lord. As the heavens are higher than the earth, so are my ways higher than your ways and my thoughts than your thoughts." So if we believe God loves us, is omniscient, and His ways and thoughts are so much higher than ours, shouldn't we expect Him to answer our prayers in ways that are best for us and are in accordance with His will?

Solomon (Ask God for Something)

God's response to our request seems to depend on our attitude, relationship with Him, His will for us, our humbleness, and similar characteristics.

I came to this conclusion when I considered Solomon's request in the Bible. When he became king of Israel, he humbled himself as a child before God—even though he was about twenty years old. He turned to the Lord for help. He asked God for a discerning heart to govern God's people and to distinguish between right and wrong (see 1 Kings 3:9).

In response to that request God said,

> Since you have asked for this and not for long life or wealth for yourself, nor have asked for the death of your enemies but for discernment in administering justice, I will do what you have asked. I will give you a wise and discerning heart, so that there will never have been anyone like you, nor will there ever be. Moreover, I will give you what you have not asked for—both wealth and honor—so that in your lifetime you will have no equal among kings. (1 Kings 3:11–13 NIV)

A beautiful example of the discernment God gave Solomon is given in 1 Kings 3:16–27. It tells of two prostitutes who came to Solomon with a problem. Both of the mothers lived in the same house, and both of them had babies. One mother said that during the night the other mother lay on her child and the child died. The other mother took the dead child and switched it with her. When she got up the next morning to feed her child, she found him dead. After looking at him closely she noticed that the child was not hers. Each mother insisted that the living child belong to herself. King Solomon requested a sword and gave instructions to cut the living child in half and give each mother one-half. The real mother of the child had compassion for the child and asked that the child be saved from death and be given to the other mother. However, the other mother said to divide the child so neither mother would have the child. King Solomon said not to kill the child but give him to the rightful mother—the first one (the mother who wanted to spare the child's life).

Another example of Solomon's wisdom involves the queen of Sheba. She did not expect King Solomon to have the knowledge and the achievements she had heard about. So she went to Jerusalem to test him with hard questions. All of the questions she asked were not hard for King Solomon to answer. After she saw his wisdom and his surroundings, she said that all that people had said about him was true. Her response was, "I did not believe what they said until I came and saw with my own eyes. Indeed, not even half the greatness of your wisdom was told me; you have far exceeded the report I heard" (2 Chronicles 9:6 NIV).

The detailed description of queen of Sheba's visit with King Solomon in 2 Chronicles 9:1–9 can be used as another example for correlating expectations and belief. She must have expected him to have some wisdom, because she went to see him to test him with hard questions. However, based on the information in verses 4–6, she did not expect King Solomon to perform at the level he did, even though her people had told her of his wisdom. She said what her people had told her about King Solomon was true. But she did not believe what they had said until she saw with her own eyes. Furthermore, she said that what they had told her about his wisdom—at least what she understood—was less than one-half of what she found his wisdom to be.

Since she acted on the expectation she had of King Solomon, it seems as if she had little faith in him. For during her visit she determined that he far exceeded her expectations—to the point that she was overwhelmed and made a pledge of periodic monetary support to him. Isn't this similar to the expectations some people have of God? Once we get to know Him better, we realize His thoughts are not our thoughts and His ways are not our ways. As the heavens are higher than the earth, so His ways and thoughts are higher than ours (see Isaiah 55:8–9). Also, we may realize that He "is able to do exceeding abundantly above all that we ask or think according to the power that worketh in us" (Ephesians 3:20 KJV).

CHAPTER 5

Family

Husband and Wife Relationship

Suppose you asked a wife if she trusted her husband, and she replied yes—or no. What would her answer tell you about that relationship? Probably not much! Why? Because the question was too general and your basis, expectation, or understanding of trust may have been different from hers. If you also asked her if she trusted her beautician, would you expect her to consider trust in the same way as she considered trust toward her husband?

Even if you made the question more specific about her husband and asked if she trusted her husband to be faithful to her, the response could be misleading. Why? Because she may have considered the word *faithful* differently than you do. Likewise if you asked the question, Do you think your husband would commit adultery? Again, you may not have learned much—because you could not tell if the response was based on the physical or mental act of committing adultery.

In other words, the word *trust* must be used in conjunction with a particular situation for good communication between persons.

The wife's responses to the questions above would have been based on her understanding of the question and on her knowledge, experience, and circumstances with her husband. Also, as shown by the questions above, her response would have been affected by her knowledge and experiences with other men—especially those she knew personally.

Trust, as defined earlier in chapter 1, is a confident expectation of someone or something. So the wife's answers would probably have been quick summaries of her knowledge, experiences, and circumstances with her husband. Her summary might have included thoughts like, *My husband treats me with respect and shows his love toward me. He is a Christian and practices his faith in God. I have not seen my husband act inappropriately around other women. I have not found any suspicious telephone numbers. He does not go to bars or similar places where he could be tempted by other women.* The list of reasons could be many—or few. If she had thought about this subject is the past and concluded that her husband was faithful to her and met other criteria she considered important for a husband to be trustworthy, then no thought summary would be necessary for her to answer the questions.

For example, after my wife and I had been married a couple of years, I received a telephone call from a man who asked me if I knew where my wife was. Immediately my response was something like, What difference does it make to you? I did not make a quick summary, and I don't even remember thinking about her trustworthiness. Even though she was a nurse, she had never given me any indication that she fit into the category that some people gave nurses.

Trust in a marriage is very important. As a matter of fact, trust is important in any relationship. Therefore, you should do your best to live a life that represents the true you and look for the truth in others you want a relationship with. I tell my grandchildren there are three things they can do to get people to trust them—tell the truth, do what you say you are going to do, and do what you are told to do as long as it is not illegal or immoral.

For a relationship that could result in marriage, it is important for a man and a woman to define their expectations of each other before they get married. Love at first sight may sound romantic, but positive expectations of each partner are very important for a marriage to last.

When a man and a woman meet, they each expect something from the other person. As a matter of fact, when they see each other before they meet, they expect something—even if one of the two may be expecting the other to leave him or her alone or not speak. More than likely each has different expectations of the other. One person may be interested in a relationship that could culminate in marriage, while the other person may expect the relationship to be no more than just friends, or to just be intimate.

One purpose of dating is to determine what is expected of each other. Achieving this purpose involves effective communication, love, patience, truthfulness, commitment, and similar factors. However, there are barriers to this process. For example, some people are hesitant to reveal the truth about themselves. Also, some people's expectations for achieving their personal goals may be so high that they distort the truth for their selfish purposes. Then some people may be afraid of being rejected or losing the special person ("someone") they consider to be the only one they will meet in a lifetime.

Dating should help each person establish expectations of the other on matters such as the following:

- Religion; for example, which religion they will practice
- Sexual intimacy; for example, when that should occur
- Finances; for example, how each one will contribute and how each one will spend
- Likes and dislikes, including each other
- Children; for example, how many and what responsibilities each parent will have in raising the child
- Problem resolution; for example, what process is used
- Moral issues, such as abortion
- Recreation; for example, what is considered fun and how much time should be allotted to it
- Family relationships; for example, likes and dislikes of family members on both sides

- Communications; for example, what should be discussed before actions, such as purchases, are taken
- Commitment; for example, things that would be a basis for divorce
- Habits and traditions; for example, what they are and the importance of each

Discussion of topics like this should not be the only basis for a person's expectations. The old saying, actions speak louder than words, is still true. Use your senses. If he says he doesn't smoke or drink alcohol and you smell smoke on his clothes or he has a smoker's or drinker's breath, your overall expectation of him should be adjusted likewise. One important fact you should consider is whether he is a liar. A smooth-talking liar can convince you a lie is the truth or the truth is a lie. If his being a nonsmoker and nondrinker is important to you, don't rely on your expectation that you can get him to change. Studies show that most of the time a person will not change. Also keep in mind what part of Proverbs 30:8 states—remove falsehood and lies far from me.

Ms. Sheri Stritof, a marriage expert, says "Marriage expectations can make or break a marriage."[6] She says it is important for married couples to share their expectations: "Sharing your expectations with your spouse is critical if you want a successful marriage ... One of the major barriers in communication is the unspoken expectations that a couple has of one another."

In addition to a man and a woman understanding as much as possible about each other before they marry, Christian couples should be in agreement as to how they plan to implement the advice the apostle Paul gives in Ephesians 5:22–33. In that scripture Paul says that wives should submit to their husbands as to the Lord, since the husband is the head of the wife as Christ is the head of the church, his body, of which He is the Savior. Some men and women misunderstand what Paul says in verses 22–24 even though he gives additional information in verses 25–33.

Again, past experiences and lack of knowledge of the Bible may contribute to the lack of understanding of those verses by one or both persons. Some people believe Paul says that a man should be an authoritarian over the woman. However, since the husband should love the wife as Christ loves the church, the husband should love his wife just as much. Do you think an authoritarian would give up his life freely for someone under his charge as Christ did? Paul also says that the husband should love his wife as his own body.

I think Paul is saying that a family—like any organization—needs structure. God has chosen man to be the head of the family. This is not just the apostle Paul's opinion. In the book of Genesis it says God created man and out of man He created woman to be a helper for the man. After they sinned, God told Eve, "Your desire will be for your husband, and he will rule over you" (Genesis 3:16b NIV). The Bible also says that a man will leave his father and mother and unite with his wife and they will become one flesh. How can they be one flesh if one of them wants to dominate the other and both of them do not understand the expectations of each other?

Expectations from Parent and Child Relationships

As expectations are important in husband and wife relationships, expectations are also important in parent and child relationships.

What should a parent expect from a child? And what should a child expect from a parent? It would be interesting to know how many parents and older children have asked themselves these questions.

Okay, fathers and mothers—and fathers- and mothers-to-be—what should you expect from your child? Again, if we refer to the Bible, Ephesians 6:1–3, it says that children should obey their parents in the Lord, for this is right. Also, the Bible says that children should honor their father and mother, which is the first commandment with a promise. Basically, we think only younger children are required to obey and honor their parents. However, to obey and honor parents are two very important things that children of all ages should do.

Adult children have additional requirements. They should show respect, or be submissive to, those who are older (see 1 Peter 5:5). Also, they should care for their parents and grandparents: "But if a widow has children or grandchildren, these should learn first of all to put their religion into practice by caring for their own family and so repaying their parents and grandparents, for this is pleasing to God" (1 Timothy 5:4 NIV).

To show the significance of children obeying parents, consider the instructions given in the Old Testament of the Bible, Deuteronomy 21:18–21 (NIV):

> If someone has a stubborn and rebellious son who does not obey his father and mother and will not listen to them when they discipline him, his father and mother shall take hold of him and bring him to the elders at the gate of his town. They shall say to the elders, "This son of ours is stubborn and rebellious. He will not obey us. He is a glutton and a drunkard." Then all the men of his town arc to stone him to death. You must purge the evil from among you. All Israel will hear of it and be afraid.

Of course, that level of punishment is not appropriate today.

Since children should obey and honor their parents, the parents' instructions to—and expectations of—their children should be realistic. Do not expect a two-year-old to act like a six-year-old, and do not expect a fifteen-year-old teenager to act like a mature person, even though he thinks he is. That means parents should assign responsibilities to children according to the age and maturity of the child. Also remember that all children do not mature at the same rate—even children of the same parents. Therefore, a parent's expectation of a child to perform at a particular level should change as the child grows in maturity.

There is a difference when it comes to what children should expect from their parents. The apostle Paul says in Ephesians 6:4 that fathers should not provoke or exasperate their children but bring them up in the training and instruction of the Lord.

In fulfilling the need for training and instructions from parents to children, there are some things parents can do.

Teach. Diligently teach the children principles that will help them be successful in life. God told the Israelites to teach their children the commandments He had given them. They were to talk about the commandments when they sat at home, when they walked along the road, when they lay down, and when they got up. They were to write them on the door frames of their houses and on their gates and tie them as symbols on their hands and bind them on their foreheads (see Deuteronomy 6:6–9).

Correct. Disciplining children has gotten to be a controversial topic. This may be because there is a fine line between discipline and abuse. However, when children are disciplined out of love, the results are advantageous. Discipline should never be administered when a parent is angry.

The wise King Solomon gives the following advice on disciplining children:

- "Whoever spares the rod hates their children, but the one who loves their children is careful to discipline them" (Proverbs 13:24 NIV).
- "Discipline your children, for in that there is hope; do not be a willing party to their death" (Proverbs 19:18 NIV).
- "Folly is bound up in the heart of a child, but the rod of discipline will drive it far away" (Proverbs 22:15 NIV).
- "Do not withhold discipline from a child; if you punish them with the rod, they will not die" (Proverbs 23:13 NIV).

Discipline should be administered with a particular purpose in mind—usually to correct a problem. The child should clearly know why he or she is being disciplined. If a child does something that the parents have identified as wrong, shouldn't the child expect some type of discipline? If the child does not get discipline, or a logical explanation, what are the parents teaching the child? A parent should also praise a child when the child is obedient and does what is right.

Train. Many people are familiar with what the Bible says in Proverbs 22:6 (KJV): "Train up a child in the way he should go: and when he is old, he will not depart from it." This topic came up in a discussion we were having in a Bible study session in a minimum security prison. One inmate seemed to have a problem with this verse, probably because he was raised in a Christian home and now was in prison. I believe the Lord had me ask him one question: "Where are you now?" The first time I asked him the question, he replied, "In prison." Immediately I asked him the same question, he and others in the class seemed to have realized the answer. (Did you get the answer?) He was in a Bible study class and had volunteered to be there. He had not departed totally from his earlier training.

Provisions. "Behold, the third time I am ready to come to you; and I will not be burdensome to you: for I seek not yours, but you: for the children ought not to lay up for the parents, but the parents for the children" (2 Corinthians 12:14 KJV).

Control. This is another area that seems to have changed in the last few decades—from my observations and comments I have heard from older people. Children seem to be controlling the parents rather than vice versa. The Bible says in 1 Timothy 3:4, 12 (NKJV), "[O]ne who rules his own house well, having his children in submission with all reverence ... Let deacons be the husbands of one wife, ruling their children and their own houses well." Although these verses are part of the qualifications for overseer and deacons, they are good advice for parents.

Love. Love is one of the most important things that children expect from parents. Children need love to grow physically and spiritually. They need love to grow healthy self-esteem, confidence, relationships, and many additional character builders. Children need love to build positive expectations of people.

The love chapter of the Bible, 1 Corinthians 13, is a beautiful description of love. Consider a few verses from that chapter, verses 4–7 and 13 (NIV). "Love is patient, love is kind. It does not envy, it does not boast, it is not proud. It does not dishonor others, it is not self-seeking, it is not easily angered, it keeps no record of wrongs. Love does not delight in evil but rejoices with the truth. It always protects, always trusts, always hopes, always perseveres ... And now these three remain: faith, hope and love. But the greatest of these is love."

Example. Someone has said that children learn more from what they see than from what they hear. From my experience I believe that is true. Because of this truth, parents should be careful of their actions. Children will learn from good actions as well as from bad actions.

Consistency. This is very important. Children need and want to know their boundaries/limits. I think having no clear-cut boundaries/limits causes a child to be frustrated. That which is not okay one time should also not be okay the next time, unless there is growth in the child and the parent explains why it is okay now and for the next time. Children expect and should receive affirmation when they do good and correction when they act wrongfully.

Truth. Many years ago a radio disk jockey ended his program with the statement, "If you always tell the truth, you don't have to remember what you said." This helps with being consistent. If you tell a child you are going to do something, do your best to do it. If you don't, the child may think that you did not tell the truth, which could result in the child not believing you the next time. Truth is a foundation for trust, and trust is a very important ingredient in all relationships.

When our children were growing up, I knew that trust between parents and children was important but I didn't know how to build that trust. I knew that if children learned to trust their parents, they would have an easier time learning to trust God; it would also improve parent-child relationships. One thing we asked them to do is memorize Proverbs 3:5–6 (KJV): "Trust in the LORD with all thine heart; and lean not unto thine own understanding. In all thy ways acknowledge him, and he shall direct thy paths." We are also emphasizing that to our grandchildren.

The things just described above that parents can teach their children may help when a parent sees a child voicing and acting out beliefs that the parent knows will lead the child into trouble. The parent may say, listen to me ... believe me ... "trust" me ... I am telling you things that are best for you. (Doesn't it seem that is what God says to us at times?) At the same time the parent may say, What can I do to get my child to "trust" me, to have realistic expectations of me?

That is when *you* must put into practice Proverbs 3:5–6. Carry out your duties as a Christian parent (some duties are mentioned above and in chapter 8 of this book), and let God lead you in the right path. Results may not come when you want them, but if you are faithful to God, a change will come.

Children are a blessing from God. That blessing can also be a joy if the child knows what to expect from the parent and the parent knows what to expect from the child. Yes, there will be grievous times; for example, when discipline is being administered and when some disagreements occur during the teenage years. Even those times cannot overshadow love shown by the family members.

Expectations of a Father

Since our expectations are based on our knowledge, experiences, and circumstances—mainly our experiences—what can a child expect from a heavenly Father if she was raised in a home without an earthly father present in the household? How can she love a heavenly Father if she has not experienced love from an earthly father? These are somewhat rhetorical questions, because many children have been reared and will be reared in homes without fathers, and sometimes without mothers. Likewise, there are homes with fathers present that do more harm to the healthy development of a child than homes without fathers.

Fathers can affect the expectations of their children positively or negatively. Could that be one reason Satan seems to be attacking families, especially the men? Satan's attacks are frustrating the roles, or responsibilities, of each family member.

So what is the responsibility/purpose of the man? What is the purpose of the woman? What is the purpose of the children? These are basic question for successful planning of a family. As an analogy, use the construction of a building. If you are told to construct a building, you will need to know the purpose of the building. Will it be used to store supplies, provide shelter for a pet, be a person's home, or another purpose? Sometimes these questions are taken for granted and people normally state the purpose with their request—or the listener assumes what the speaker means. Also, when the purpose is not evident, the listener may ask questions like, What are you going to do with that? or Why do you need that?

Let's use the Bible to show God's original purposes of man, woman, and marriage. Genesis 1:26 (NIV) states that God made man in His image to "rule over the fish in the sea and the birds in the sky, over the livestock and all the wild animals, and over all the creatures that move along the ground." Not only was man created to rule over many things, he was to work the ground and take care of the things God had created. Some people say God created man in His image so that men (and women) may have fellowship with Him. God created woman from man to be a helper suitable for the man.

God created man and woman to "Be fruitful and increase in number; fill the earth and subdue it. Rule over the fish in the sea and the birds in the sky and over every living creature that moves on the ground" (Genesis 1:28 NIV). The man is supposed to "leave his father and mother and be joined to his wife, and they shall become one flesh" (Genesis 2:24 NKJV).

After the first man and woman sinned, their purposes were adjusted.

> To the woman he said, "I will make your pains in childbearing very severe; with painful labor you will

> give birth to children. Your desire will be for your husband, and he will rule over you." To Adam he said, "Because you listened to your wife and ate fruit from the tree about which I commanded you, 'You must not eat from it,' Cursed is the ground because of you; through painful toil you will eat food from it all the days of your life. It will produce thorns and thistles for you, and you will eat the plants of the field. By the sweat of your brow you will eat your food until you return to the ground, since from it you were taken; for dust you are and to dust you will return." (Genesis 3:16–19 NIV)

So the adjusted primary purpose of man was to work for the food, and the wife was to give birth to children so that their numbers would increase. Now the purposes of the man, woman, and children seem to be different in many homes. Men and women are working outside of the home for the "food." Many times this situation leaves little time for the parents to raise their children. To compensate for not having time for the children, the parents tend to give the children material possessions and less discipline. Less, or inconsistent, discipline results in children not having definite boundaries between right and wrong, resulting in frustration for the children. Frustrations can yield anger, fear, abuse, retaliation, dishonor, hate, defiance, rebellion, and many other undesirable characteristics, not just for the children but for the parents as well. Then the expectations of each family member can be more negative than positive.

I am not saying that working outside the home will have disastrous or negative results for all husbands and wives. But it does present a challenge for the family. For many years when our children were young, my wife and I worked outside the home, but the Lord helped us to keep the amount of time to a minimum when our children were not with at least one of us. Most of our activities were centered around the development of our children rather than our individual pleasure. For example, we did not look at television during the children's study time. As a matter of fact, we did not own a television for several years.

Social media and the advancement of electronics have introduced serious challenges to present-day families.

Children raised in homes where all members feel they are loved; where the children receive proper discipline, not abuse, in a consistent manner; where communications are effective; where each member's role, or purpose, is clearly evident and understood; and where God is understood to be number One, will have a good chance of accepting God as their heavenly Father. Again, I understand all of these conditions are not necessary for a child to accept God as his Father. However, all parents should strive to raise their children in the conditions mentioned in the first part of this section to help develop families this world needs and to fulfill our purpose in this world.

The Sweet Potato Lesson

One year my wife, Celestine, decided to plant some sweet potato plants in two large containers. Because of a dry summer we did not always keep the soil moist; therefore, we didn't know what to expect when she thought it was time to dig the potatoes. To our surprise the plants had some medium and small potatoes. Some of the small potatoes were long and skinny, and some were short and chubby.

One time when she was preparing to bake some of the potatoes, I asked her to include some of the small potatoes, which she did. Since we were not used to cooking long and skinny potatoes, we did not check them in time to see if they had finished cooking, so some of the long and skinny potatoes were cooked too much; they "burned."

One morning when I came into the kitchen, I noticed the sweet potatoes that had been left on the stove and decided to eat a small one, one that was skinny. Of course it was burned too much for me to eat. A thought came to me, a spiritual revelation: what happened to the potatoes can represent what can happen to Christians.

When a person accepts Christ as his Lord and Savior, he can be compared to the skinny potato. There is not much meat in his

Christianity. He needs someone to look after him until he grows in his relationship with God. He can withstand the "heat" of Satan's attacks and temptations for only a short time.

The fatter sweet potatoes did not burn. Even the smaller potatoes that were short and chubby were edible. This presents another analogy to Christianity. Those Christians who are babes in Christ should concentrate on studying God's Word and putting what they learn into practice. If they try to spread themselves too thin by trying to do so much for Christ without growing in His Word, they could become easy targets for Satan.

There is another spiritual lesson to learn from the baking of the sweet potatoes. If you see people under the *heat* of Satan, try to rescue them before they get *burned*. Even Christians need reminding where their focus should be, because they can think they are stronger (fatter) than they really are and fall for Satan's lies. The apostle Paul says in 1 Corinthians 10:12–13 (KJV), "Wherefore let him that thinketh he standeth take heed lest he fall. There hath no temptation taken you but such as is common to man: but God is faithful, who will not suffer you to be tempted above that ye are able; but will with the temptation also make a way to escape, that ye may be able to bear it." Note that God makes a way for Christians to escape the temptation, but He leaves it up to us to choose that escape. That is why a person may need another person to help him or her to see how to get out of the temptation.

Just as we cannot expect large, small, and skinny sweet potatoes to finish cooking sufficiently at the same time, we cannot expect all Christians to have the same level of faith and relationships with God. So what are your expectations of Christians? Do you expect Christians to not make mistakes—sin? Do you expect all Christians to act the same way, to interpret and explain the Bible the same way, to dress the same way, etc.? I hope not, because God made us all different and unique and gave us a free will to choose and make decisions, wise or foolish. However, free will does not allow us to do anything we want; there are limitations. For example, we cannot choose to fly like a bird without man-made assistance. We cannot choose to walk through a solid wall. And we cannot choose things that are not in God's will/ plan and expect to receive all the blessings He originally had for us.

Racial Expectations

What are your expectations of another race of people? How did you get those expectations? Are they predominately positive or negative views? When you see a person for the first time, what categories do you put them in? Do you find yourself putting the person in some of these categories—race, old or young, level of wealth, pleasing to the eye or not, intelligent or not, friend or foe, geographical region they may be from, a prey or not, religious person or not, law enforcement or not, etc.? Have you wondered why the color of a person's skin, the shape of his eyes, the texture of his hair, the way he speaks, and other characteristics affect your expectation of someone, or the particular race of the person?

In America there seems to be a continuing division between the black, or African American, race and the white, or Caucasian, race. This continuation seems to be occurring even though laws have been created in an attempt to correct the problem. Laws to integrate schools, workplaces, public events, transportation, purchasing of homes, etc., have helped, but have they changed the individual expectations that persons have of races different from theirs?

While using the Internet to prepare for a Bible study lesson on the subject "God of All Nations," I read an interesting article by a person who wanted to change his or her view on blacks. The person said he or she was not a member of a radical racial group, didn't condone racial violence, and didn't think all blacks were inferior or genetically less intelligent. However, some of the writer's views of blacks were as follows:

- They act rudely or inappropriately in public
- They have a very high incarceration rate and therefore are more likely to commit crimes
- They have lower achievement in school

- The likelihood of him or her having a negative experience when dealing with a black person was higher than with other races.

Where do people get expectations like these? Do you think they are taught these expectations? Two of the likely sources are people who influence them and the media. Just think about the news you read in the newspapers and see on television and the Internet. Showing pictures of people who commit crimes and the punishment they receive could influence the expectations of people who do not have a personal relationship with the race of people whose pictures are being shown.

Wouldn't America be a better country if each of us could be convinced like the apostle Peter was in chapter 10 of Acts? Being a Jew, Peter had difficulty accepting Gentiles, non-Jews, into the early Christian church. God gave Peter a vision three times about killing and eating animals that Peter thought were unclean. He then arranged for Peter to go see Cornelius, a non-Jew centurion who had been visited by an angel, and who was expecting Peter. The experience convinced/convicted Peter to exclaim, "I now realize how true it is that God does not show favoritism but accepts from every nation the one who fears him and does what is right" (Acts 10:34–35 NIV). What would it take to convince/convict us to not show favoritism? What are we doing to change our expectations of another race or religion, to be more positive? What are we doing to help others of another race to change their negative expectations of us? The challenge is not easy and requires much work from both sides.

Expectations for Teenagers Who Want to "Leave" Home.

There are times when children think that living at home is so bad that they would like to leave home and live elsewhere. This could be true for any socioeconomic conditions of the home. There are homes where the living conditions are so bad that the child would have a "legitimate" reason to leave home. However, some children living in a home feel they are not getting what they deserve and can do better living somewhere else. No matter what the reason for wanting to "leave home," the decision to "leave home" is a major decision. It needs to be considered very carefully by the teenager, and the consequences need to be explained lovingly, if possible, by a caregiver.

There are many *vultures* just waiting for these immature young people to become available for their immoral and possible illegal use of the teens. The *vultures* are experienced in knowing how and what to promise the teenagers, and show them "*love*," in order to get them to come under their influence and control.

Control by *vultures* is only one of the many challenges teenagers face when they decide to leave home. There are so many problems they may face that I will not try to address all of them in this book. However, I will list a few:

- Teens under the age of majority, eighteen years old in some states, may expect many more problems than teens over the age of majority.
- Some problems teens may expect depend on the reason they leave their homes; for example, if they were thrown out, experienced unbearable conditions at home, voluntarily left, and similar conditions.
- Teens, and adults, may expect legal matters to be different for minors than for adults.
- Some problems teens may expect depend on whether the teen is emancipated.
- Teens under the age of majority may be involved with child protective services and the courts if they leave home, with or without their parents' permission.

(For more information on this subject, read the "Teenagers on Their Own" section in Livia Bardin's book[7] titled *Starting Out in Mainstream America*. Available online only at http://startingout.icsa.name/ .)

In my limited research on this topic, I was surprised to learn the following: Many states frown on or even criminalize the act of helping a minor who has left home.

- These laws, intended to protect young people from being exploited by predatory adults, may backfire in cases where protection from parents truly is needed.
- *Adults who take in a youth who has left home—even though they are family members or friends—may find themselves charged with violations such as "contributing to the delinquency of a minor" or "interfering with custodial rights."* [italics added for emphasis] (Refer to: http://startingout.icsa.name/startingout/childteen/teen.)

One thing teenagers may not expect is the expenses involved with living on their own. Some of the expenses they may expect are as follows:

- A place to stay—protective services, room, apartment, etc. This could range from a few hundred dollars to thousands of dollars. Usually the less costly places are located in less appropriate places for teens.
- Necessities, such as food, toilet tissue, soap, plates, silverware, towels and washcloths, toothpaste, deodorant, powder, paper towels, etc.
- Mobile phone and service from a mobile phone provider
- School, college, and trade school expenses
- Transportation to get to and from work, school, and other places
- Health and life insurance, and maybe rental insurance
- Medical and dental expenses
- Social and entertainment expenses
- Savings

These expenses can easily add up to over $1,000 per month, in year 2015 dollars. This is critical, since more than likely the teenager's income comes from a minimum-wage job. Minimum wage in 2015 was approximately $8.00 per hour. After required deductions, the teenager may expect approximately $1,100 per month for a forty-hour-per-week job, which means the teenager must learn how to budget and control expenses to keep from becoming homeless, or coming under the control of a *vulture*.

CHAPTER 6

Decisions

Expectations of Decisions

A statement that is important to me is, *You live the decisions you make.* Let me explain why that statement is important.

Every day we make many decisions. Some have little effect on our lives, while others may have significant effects. Sometimes the consequences of our decisions are immediate, yet sometimes the consequences occur much later in life. So what should people expect from their decisions?

For example, consider the following:

- What should a person expects if he or she starts smoking cigarettes or using other tobacco products?
- What should a person expects if he or she starts stealing?
- What should a person expects if he or she starts using alcohol (as a beverage), drugs, or similar substances?
- What should a person expects if he or she eats more calories than his or her body needs?
- What should a person expects if he or she is disobedient to those in authority?

- What should a person expects if he or she breaks laws and commands? This question is different from the last question because a person can break a law without a person in authority knowing that a law has been broken.
- What should a teenager expects if he or she does not do his or her best in school?
- What should a person expect after death?

Did you give much thought to each of the questions? Probably not, especially if you have not thought about the questions before. So consider the first question, restated this way: What may a teenager expect from smoking a cigarette? Some possibilities are as follows:

- Be accepted in a desired group
- Give the appearance of being mature
- Be like a parent, role model, mentor, or someone he or she admires.
- Bad breath at times
- Addiction to tobacco products
- Costly habit—to purchase products and later, medical bills
- Increased susceptibility to respiratory illness
- Shortness of breath
- Impaired lung growth and function
- Foul-smelling clothes, automobile, home, etc.—foul-smelling to nonsmokers
- Lung, mouth, throat, kidney, and stomach cancers
- Coronary heart disease
- Emphysema and other chronic diseases
- Significantly reduced life span
- Increased medical bills

The immediate physical consequences/effects of smoking the first cigarette may be minimal. If so, the teenager's expectations of the negative effects of smoking cigarettes may also be minimal. This attitude could lead the teenager to continue smoking until it becomes an addiction. If the teenager decided to stop smoking cigarettes after smoking the first one, the decision to smoke the first cigarette may have little effect on his or her life. However, if the teenager continued to smoke or use other tobacco products throughout his or her life, the results may be significant—like the more devastating possibilities in the above list. The teenager will live the decisions he or she makes. The teenager may expect the consequences now, later, or both.

The decisions a teenager may make concerning smoking a cigarette is an example of the factors involved in any decision any of us makes. If we consider more factors, we improve our possibilities of reaping better results. Keep in mind that Satan wants us to look only at the present situation and consider just a few factors. If you consider a lot of factors and look at the future and see the consequences of your decision today, you may decide not to yield to his (Satan's) temptation.

Many times people may not stop to think about the consequences when they make a decision. If they don't think about the consequences, how will they know what to truly expect? Most of us probably believe we are making the right decision at the time we make the decision. However, a person may have biased, selfish, or insufficient information on which to base the decision. Therefore, it is important for him or her to seek advice or opinions from trusted relatives, friends, and/or experts, especially for decisions that could have a major impact on his or her life. Also, it is important to listen to the advice of trusted relatives and friends even if he or she does not ask them for advice. Of course, we should always seek godly wisdom and knowledge.

Expectations Affect Decisions

Just as we go through each day without giving much thought about what we expect, we also do not give much thought about how many decisions we make. However, consciously or unconsciously, we have to make many decisions each day in this life. As was stated in the last section, "You live the decisions you make."

We are constantly determining what we should or should not do or say. For example, do we get out of the bed, or do we sleep in? What clothes should we put on? Whom should we marry, or should we stay single? Who or what should be my god—we will worship someone or something. The list could be endless.

However, I think our expectation(s) of each option of a choice will be instrumental in the decision we make, including the expectation of the consequences of each option.

Consider the choice of getting out of bed. If we are living an exciting well-ordered life, are in good health, have a good job, and similar conditions, getting out of bed may not seem to be a choice to make. It seems natural. However, if we are not prepared to make an important decision that day or if getting out of bed will make us feel worse, or if we have a job we don't like going to, then we have to consider our expectations, including consequences. Do we expect that staying in bed will improve or worsen the consequences?

An example from the Bible can show how expectations can affect a person's choice. The quoted verses below for this example are selected verses from 2 Kings 5 (NIV).

> Now Naaman was commander of the army of the king of Aram. He was a great man in the sight of his master and highly regarded, because through him the LORD had given victory to Aram. He was a valiant soldier, but he had leprosy.
>
> Now bands of raiders from Aram had gone out and had taken captive a young girl from Israel, and she served Naaman's wife. She said to her mistress, "If only my master would see the prophet who is in Samaria! He would cure him of his leprosy" (vv. 1–3).

Naaman got permission from his master to visit the prophet the captive young girl had suggested. The prophet was Elisha.

Naaman went with his horses and chariots and stopped at the door of Elisha's house. Elisha did not come to the door but sent a messenger to tell him, "Go, wash yourself seven times in the Jordan, and your flesh will be restored and you will be cleansed."

> But Naaman went away angry and said, "I thought that he would surely come out to me and stand and call on the name of the LORD his God, wave his hand over the spot and cure me of my leprosy. Are not Abana and Pharpar, the rivers of Damascus, better than all the waters of Israel? Couldn't I wash in them and be cleansed?" So he turned and went off in a rage.
>
> Naaman's servants went to him and said, "My father, if the prophet had told you to do some great thing, would you not have done it? How much more, then, when he tells you, 'Wash and be cleansed'!" So he went down and dipped himself in the Jordan seven times, as the man of God had told him, and his flesh was restored and became clean like that of a young boy (vv. 10–14, NIV).

What future could a commander of an army, a great and highly respected man in the sight of his master, and a valiant soldier, Naaman, expect if he had leprosy? Not much, because leprosy was a dreaded disease that could result in the person being an outcast until death.

So when he learned that there might be someone who could cure his disease, his expectations for the future probably increased significantly. This is evident in the amount of goods he took to give to Elisha, who he expected would cure his leprosy—ten talents of silver (about 750 pounds), six thousand shekels of gold (about 150 pounds), and ten sets of clothing.

What did Naaman expect from Elisha? He expected Elisha to come out to him and stand and call on the name of the Lord his God, wave his hand over the spot, and cure him of his leprosy. What did Elisha do? He sent a messenger to say to Naaman, go wash yourself seven times in the Jordan.

Since Naaman did not get what he expected, he chose not to follow Elisha's instructions but chose to be angry and went off in a rage.

Fortunately for Naaman, he had servants who cared for him enough to show him the error in his thinking. His expectations changed again, and this time he made the correct choice. Naaman was obedient to Elisha's instructions and went down and dipped himself in the Jordan seven times—then his flesh was restored and became clean like that of a young boy. In addition to the physical healing, Naaman seemed to have received a spiritual healing too.

Expectations from Sensitivity and Sensuality

If a person is not careful, he or she may make the transition from sensitivity to sensuality without even expecting the resulting outcome. Even though there may be many signs to "warn" a person of the change, he may ignore or excuse the signs. The following discussion helps to explain the process.

While I was preparing a Bible study lesson for a group of men, the Lord revealed to me a beautiful explanation of how someone can change from acting *good* to acting *bad*. The scripture is found in the fourth chapter of Ephesians, where the apostle Paul was telling Christians how to live. In the seventeenth verse he said that Christians should no longer live as the Gentiles did, for they were futile in their thinking. Here *Gentiles* refer to the unsaved, or heathens.

Paul explained one futility of the unsaved thinking in the nineteenth verse: "Having lost all sensitivity, they have given themselves over to sensuality so as to indulge in every kind of impurity, and they are full of greed" (v. 19 NIV). To get a better understanding of what Paul was saying, consider the definitions of two key words, *sensitivity* and *sensuality*.

Sensitivity can be defined as the quality of being capable of responding to the stimulation of one or more of the senses, whereas sensuality may be defined as the quality of being preoccupied with the gratification of the physical appetites. Consider again the first part of the nineteenth verse: "Having lost all sensitivity, they have given themselves over to sensuality." By using the definitions of the two words, this phrase can be summarized as, Without being capable of responding to the stimulation of one or more of the senses, they have given themselves over to being preoccupied with the gratification of the physical appetites.

Consider several examples. Suppose parents raise a child to know that stealing is wrong. When that child is away from his or her parents and the temptation to steal presents itself, the child may receive a stimulation to not steal. If the child overrides that stimulation and steals, the follow-on temptations to steal will be met with less stimulation on each occurrence. At some point the child may be preoccupied with a desire to steal.

Likewise, an adult can go through a similar process when faced with the temptation to commit adultery, lie, steal, consume drugs, lust, love others more than God, and other actions. Christians need to work hard not to lose that sensitivity to do right, rather than to do wrong. For this may be God's way of telling them when they are being tempted to do evil. One of Satan's objectives is to get a Christian to go from being sensitive to being sensual.

The last paragraph lists some things that Satan can entice Christians to do that they should not. Similarly, there are some things that Christians should do that Satan can entice them to not do. Christians can start reading their Bible and have devotions every day and participate in Bible study one or more times a week. When they don't read and study, they feel like something is missing for the day or week. Something may happen to distract them from reading the Bible and devotion for a day. They see that they have *more time* to get *some rest*, get to work earlier, or something similar that would reduce their sensitivity. Slowly the Bible reading and Bible study are reduced until they are not doing either on a regular basis. Therefore, periodically, Christians need to review their sensitivity to Bible and religious reading, church attendance, tithing, Sunday school participation, and similar activities to keep them from deteriorating to the sensual level.

Years ago I came to love the twentieth verse in chapter 4 of Ephesians: "But ye have not so learned Christ" (KJV). This was a turning point where the apostle Paul stopped saying what Christians should not do and started telling us what to do. Now I can use the nineteenth verse, referenced above, to better expect and understand the actions of some people, especially young adults who were raised in Christian homes.

To me, many young people do not establish a personal spiritual relationship with God until they become *independent* of their parents or guardians. They know what their parents have told them, and they have seen their parents "practice" their religion. Until the young adults' independence, they may or may not have put their parents' religion to a test to determine the validity of their parents' faith. When young adults are making the transition of becoming independent, they are more vulnerable to Satan's temptations. Even though they may have a strong sensitivity to do right, corrupt environments and distractions can encourage them to lose that sensitivity.

Also, I think hypocritical parents can cause the sensitivity of the child to be weak. Under those conditions a child may not learn what is right and what is wrong. When parents say to do what they say rather than what they do, the child may probably think the parents do not believe what they are saying. A young person seems to learn more from imitation than from listening. There is some truth is the saying "Action speaks louder than words." Likewise, if parents don't encourage children to be accountable for their actions, the sensitivity of the children to do right may be weak. This also seems to be true for adults.

Christian parents who spend a lot of time doing "church" work rather than spending quality time with their children may damage the children's desire to be sensitive to do right. Likewise, Christian parents who work on their job(s) more than they have to—so their children can have more than what they, the parents, had when they were young—may not pass on the faith that their parents passed on to them.

Young Christians who have recently accepted the Lord as their Savior should expect to face temptations for them to hold onto the ways of their old self, their former ways. It is important for these Christians to find friends and environments that will encourage them to improve in their faith in God and in their sensitivity to do right.

Remember, love for God and others is the primary building block for sensitivity. Love for self is the primary building block for sensuality.

CHAPTER 7

Prosperity

Wealth Affects Expectations

Are you affected by your wealth, or as you may think, lack of wealth? Are you sure? When you buy a car or clothing, what motivates you to select the car or clothing you purchase? Do you find yourself asking why an organization or church does not treat you a certain way because of the amount of money you give them? Do you say that you cannot tithe because you don't have enough money?

The Bible has much to say about how resources may affect a person's expectations. A few examples will illustrate this point.

A landowner hired some men to work in his vineyard. He hired some men early in the morning and agreed to pay them a denarius, a usual daily wage. He likewise hired some men at midmorning, noon, midafternoon, and even some soon before quitting time. The landowner told the men he hired after the early morning that he would pay them whatever was right (see Matthew 20:1–16). If you were one of those workmen, what would you expect?

Well, at the end of the day the landowner paid them all the same amount, one denarius—including the ones who came early in the morning as well as those who came one hour before quitting time. Those men who worked all day had expected to receive more than the others. Note that the landowner made an agreement on a wage with only the first group. With the others he agreed to pay whatever was right.

Another example showing how resources may affect a person involves a young man who asked Jesus what he must do to receive eternal life. Jesus told him to obey the commandments. After the young man said that he kept the commandments, Jesus told him if he wanted to be perfect he needed to sell his possessions, give to the poor, and then follow Him. This response made the young man go away sad, because he was wealthy (see Matthew 19:16–22). It seems like the young man's expectations changed significantly during his conversation with Jesus.

When our friends Robert and Deborah Rose were stationed in Germany during his military service, my wife, Celestine, thought that would be a good time to get her dream car, a popular German-made car. They could arrange to purchase the car in Germany and send it to us in Virginia. Shortly before we were married I had purchased my dream car, a Thunderbird. Since she was working and had helped to educate our children, I agreed with her to get the car. Also, I had heard that Germany was known for its quality equipment.

Even though the car had many good features, it repeatedly required a lot of maintenance, and the maintenance was quite expensive. For example, a replacement battery for that car cost approximately six times the cost of batteries I replaced in my other vehicle.

We kept the car for ten years expecting the maintenance to improve; however, it got worse. After we traded the car for one made by a different manufacturer, Celestine shared with me that she thought the Holy Spirit had told her to get rid of the car much earlier.

God had allowed us to get the German-made car, which we expected to last many years; but it didn't last as long as we expected. Also, we did not expect the car to put us in a higher social class, but it seemed to have done that. In general, we did not voluntarily tell our relatives and friends we had bought the German-made car. However, some relatives said we were rich. So it seemed that the car also changed the expectations of others toward us.

Do people trust richer people more than poorer people? Do they expect richer people to treat them better than poorer people? If a shabbily dressed person comes into a store just after a well-dressed person—where there is no formed line—which one would you expect to receive service first? Even if both of those persons would go into a place of worship, would you expect both to receive the same reception? If you have not observed who gets preferential treatment, try watching people who are serving customers and see who gets served first. Better yet, observe whom you tend to serve first.

Expectations and Needs

Sometimes our expectations are based on our needs and on what we think other people can provide. The Bible gives good examples of this.

> One day Peter and John were going up to the temple at the time of prayer—at three in the afternoon. Now a man who was lame from birth was being carried to the temple gate called Beautiful, where he was put every day to beg from those going into the temple courts. When he saw Peter and John about to enter, he asked them for money. Peter looked straight at him, as did John. Then Peter said, "Look at us!" So the man gave them his attention, expecting to get something from them.
>
> Then Peter said, "Silver or gold I do not have, but what I do have I give you. In the name of Jesus Christ of Nazareth, walk." Taking him by the right hand, he helped him up, and instantly the man's feet and ankles became strong. He jumped to his feet and began to walk. Then he went with them into the temple

> courts, walking and jumping, and praising God. (Acts 3:1–8 NIV)

What did the crippled man expect from Peter and John? He expected money from the *church-going* people. Not only did he expect money from Peter and John, he expected money from anyone who would give it to him. He had a need. He was over forty years old and had been crippled from birth, not by an accident.

What did Peter and John expect? They expected God to perform a miracle on the crippled man. They expected the man to get up and walk. They not only expected the man to be healed and then learn to walk, but to instantly go from being crippled—depending on someone to carry him to the temple—to being able to walk on his own. Peter and John had what the man really needed, physical healing. In addition to being healed physically, the man may have also been healed spiritually.

Did the crippled man get what he expected? Originally, no! However, he was obedient to Peter and John and got more than he originally expected. This is a good example of what we can get from God when we are obedient to Him.

Did Peter and John get what they expected from God? Yes! They may have gotten more than they had expected. They expected the man to get up and walk—but did they expect the crippled man to go with them into the temple courts and start jumping and praising God?

Envy Affects Trust/Expectations

Envy is defined as discontent with who one is or what one has and the desire to be someone else or to have what someone else has. Asaph, a musician, expressed envy very eloquently in Psalm 73:2–3 (NIV): "But as for me, my feet had almost slipped; I had nearly lost my foothold. For I envied the arrogant when I saw the prosperity of the wicked." He made these statements after acknowledging how good God is to those who have a clean heart.

Do Asaph's statements remind us of the way we think at times? When we seem to be struggling to live a Christian life with hardships, disappointments, hurts, and the lack of material possessions we think we should have, the apparent life of the rich and famous looks appealing. But consider this: do you think faithful Christians don't deserve to have hardships, disappointments, and suffering, or do you expect hardships, disappointments, and suffering to produce faithful Christians?

Here in the United States we seem to have distorted what is important, what is significant, or what is most valuable, especially when we consider education and entertainment. Many entertainers and athletics get multimillion-dollar contracts and endorsements, while our educators get relatively low salaries, with little or no annual increases. We should admire our schoolteachers. Teachers have the awesome responsibility of teaching our children the fundamentals of being effective citizens. They are expected to work long days and to personally provide supplies because the school funds are low. They are expected to deal with and correct children who bring problems from home, yet the teachers have to be very careful how they touch or hug them.

One disadvantage of envy is that you don't appreciate what you already have. This is one way it affects expectations. When you don't appreciate what you have, you are probably thinking that God has not given you what you think you should have. So when you pray for God to give you what you want and He doesn't give it to you in the way you expect Him to, you may start looking to yourself to get it your way. That attitude leads to a downfall because you start expecting less from God—who has the greater wisdom—and you expect more from yourself, who has the lesser wisdom. In other words, you trust yourself more than you trust God.

Prosperity and Success

Many people expect, or want, to be prosperous and successful. That may be one reason some people regularly play the lottery and participate in other gambling activities. To them prosperity is a measure of success. Other people would consider themselves successful if they could become powerful by becoming the CEO, or similar, in a large corporation or organization. They feel that if they knew the right people and were aggressive, they could get to the top of an organization. They set goals with timetables to reach their lofty heights of ambition.

From what I have read and heard, mature Christians, in general, would disagree with this strategy for becoming successful. They say in order to succeed, a person *should not* gamble, have a desire to be powerful, have influential friends, and be aggressive. While preparing a Bible study lesson on being successful, I received another view of the success strategy.

The difference in the general Christian view on the above strategy and the view I received is the source of the person's expectations. One reason Christians may disagree with the strategy is because they think prosperity and success do not come from someone having a desire to be powerful, having influential friends, and being aggressive. They see the source of this strategy as selfish expectations.

While this is true, there is another way of looking at the strategy. What would be wrong with the strategy if the source of the expectations is God, as revealed by the view I received? If a person expects God to supply all of his or her needs, then why would that person play the lottery? If a person is humble, unselfish, and obedient to God's Word, wouldn't that make him or her powerful? Is there an influential friend greater than God? Shouldn't a child of God have a relentless desire to study His Word and learn how to put that wisdom into action—which leads to greater success?

A good example of these two views is the apostle Paul. Before he was converted to Christianity, his name was Saul.

After Stephen, a devoted Christian disciple, was stoned to death, a great persecution was started against the church in Jerusalem. Saul was also part of the intense persecution against the church. This is what Saul said in Acts 26:9–11 (NIV):

> I too was convinced that I ought to do all that was possible to oppose the name of Jesus of Nazareth. And that is just what I did in Jerusalem. On the authority of the chief priests I put many of the Lord's people in prison, and when they were put to death, I cast my vote against them. Many a time I went from one synagogue to another to have them punished, and I tried to force them to blaspheme. I was so obsessed with persecuting them that I even hunted them down in foreign cities.

But he had a significant event to change his selfish motive—his selfish strategy:

> On one of these journeys I was going to Damascus with the authority and commission of the chief priests. About noon, King Agrippa, as I was on the road, I saw a light from heaven, brighter than the sun, blazing around me and my companions. We all fell to the ground, and I heard a voice saying to me in Aramaic, "Saul, Saul, why do you persecute me? It is hard for you to kick against the goads" (vv. 12–14).

This experience eventually led him (now named apostle Paul) to say in Philippians 3:7–9 (KJV),

> But what things were gain to me, those I counted loss for Christ. Yea doubtless, and I count all things but loss for the excellency of the knowledge of Christ Jesus my Lord: for whom I have suffered the loss of all things, and do count them but dung, that I may win Christ, And be found in him, not having mine own righteousness, which is of the law, but that which is through the faith of Christ, the righteousness which is of God by faith.

Before Paul was converted, the source of his expectations was himself. After his conversion he realized that those things he thought were important for his success were dung in comparison to the knowledge of Christ Jesus his Lord. The source of his expectations had been changed from himself to God. With God as his source of expectations he says,

> Most gladly therefore will I rather glory in my infirmities, that the power of Christ may rest upon me. Therefore I take pleasure in infirmities, in reproaches, in necessities, in persecutions, in distresses for Christ's sake: for when I am weak, then am I strong. (2 Corinthians 12:9–10 KJV)

Paul's attitude toward his strength is similar to that of John the Baptist. John said, "I baptize you with water for repentance. But after me comes one who is more powerful than I, whose sandals I am not worthy to carry. He will baptize you with the Holy Spirit and fire (Matthew 3:11, NIV).

True success is not always associated with prosperity, as we may expect. One of the most prosperous and wisest men in the Bible, Solomon, became wise and rich because he was unselfish. After Solomon offered a thousand burnt offerings on an altar, God told Solomon to ask Him for what he wanted God to give him. (If God had told you that, what would you ask Him for?) Solomon asked God for wisdom and knowledge to govern His people. God told Solomon that since he had not asked for wealth, riches, honor, death of his enemies, and a long life, he would give him wisdom, knowledge, wealth, riches, and honor that no king before and after him would have (see 2 Chronicles 1:6–12).

During his life King Solomon seems to have confirmed that wisdom, wealth, and similar successes, were not that important in life. Some theologians believe King Solomon wrote the book of Ecclesiastes in the Bible. (No writer's name is mentioned for the book. It refers only to the *Teacher.*) The author of this book records how he tried to find what is meaningful in life. He tried the things that many people would expect to be meaningful and made these observations:

- Wisdom is meaningless
- Pleasures are meaningless
- Toil is meaningless
- Advancement is meaningless
- Riches are meaningless
- Everything is meaningless

At the end of the book the *Teacher* says, "Let us hear the conclusion of the whole matter: Fear God, and keep his commandments: for this is the whole duty of man. For God shall bring every work into judgment, with every secret thing, whether it be good, or whether it be evil" (Ecclesiastes 12:13–14 KJV).

Another example in the Bible of a man with a right attitude toward prosperity and "success" is Job. He was a blameless and upright man who had a wife, seven sons, three daughters, seven thousand sheep, three thousand camels, five hundred yoke of oxen, five hundred donkeys, and a large number of servants. He was considered the greatest man of all the people of the East.

One time after Satan visited the earth, he had a discussion with God. During the discussion, "the Lord said to Satan, 'Have you considered My servant Job, that *there is* none like him on the earth, a blameless and upright man, one who fears God and shuns evil?'" (Job 1:8 NKJV). Satan told God that Job would curse Him if not for the protection God had around him (Job).

To prove to God that Job would surely curse Him to His face, Satan got permission from God to take everything from Job. Satan was instrumental in Job losing everything he had—including his children—except Job's wife and a few servants. Job's response is given in Job 1:20–22 (KJV):

> Then Job arose, and rent his mantle, and shaved his head, and fell down upon the ground, and worshipped, And said, Naked came I out of my mother's womb, and naked shall I return thither: the Lord gave, and the

> Lord hath taken away; blessed be the name of the Lord.
> In all this Job sinned not, nor charged God foolishly.

Because of Job's faithfulness, God made him prosperous again and gave him twice as much as he had before his ordeal (see Job 42:10).

One verse in the Bible is often misquoted. You may have heard the quote "Money is the root of all evil." However, the Bible does not say that. The Bible states in 1 Timothy 6:10 (KJV), "[F]or the love of money is the root of all evil." Money is not the root of evil—it becomes evil when we cherish it instead of the One who really gave the money to us.

It is not so much what we have or the position we hold, but the attitude we have toward what we have and the position we hold, and the object of our love.

CHAPTER 8

Expectations of Christians

What can people expect from Christians, or what can Christians expect of themselves? The New Testament in the Bible gives a lot of information on this topic; the twelfth chapter of Romans (NKJV) gives us a good idea.

1. "Present your bodies a living sacrifice, holy, acceptable to God, which is your reasonable service" (v. 1).
2. "Do not be conformed to this world, but be transformed by the renewing of your mind, that you may prove what is that good and acceptable and perfect will of God" (v. 2).
3. "Not to think of [yourself] more highly than [you] ought to think, but to think soberly, as God has dealt to each one a measure of faith" (v. 3).
4. "Having gifts differing according to the grace that is given to you, use them: if prophecy, prophesy in proportion to your faith; if ministry, minister; if teaching, teach; if exhortation, exhort; if giving, give liberally; if leading, lead with diligence; if showing mercy, do it with cheerfulness" (vv. 6–8 with some words deleted).
5. "Let your love be without hypocrisy" (v. 9).
6. "Abhor what is evil" (v. 9).
7. "Cling to what is good" (v. 9).

8. "Be kindly affectionate to one another with brotherly love, in honor giving preference to one another" (v. 10).
9. "Don't lag in diligence" (v. 11).
10. "Be fervent in spirit, serving the Lord" (v. 11).
11. "[Rejoice] in hope" (v. 12).
12. "[Be] patient in tribulation" (v. 12).
13. "[Continue] steadfastly in prayer" (v. 12).
14. "[Distribute] to the needs of the saints" (v. 13).
15. "[Be] given to hospitality" (v. 13).
16. "Bless those who persecute you" (v. 14).
17. "Bless and do not curse" (v. 14).
18. "Rejoice with those who rejoice" (v. 15).
19. "Weep with those who weep" (v. 15).
20. "Be of the same mind toward one another" (v. 16).
21. "Do not set your mind on high things, but associate with the humble" (v. 16).
22. "Do not be wise in your own opinion" (v. 16).
23. "Repay no one evil for evil" (v. 17).
24. "Have regard for good things in the sight of all men" (v. 17).
25. "If it is possible, as much as depends on you, live peaceably with all men" (v. 18).
26. "Do not avenge yourselves, but rather give place to wrath; for it is written, 'Vengeance is Mine, I will repay' says the Lord" (v. 19).
27. "If your enemy is hungry, feed him" (v. 20).
28. "If he is thirsty, give him a drink; for in so doing you will heap coals of fire on his head" (v. 20).
29. "Do not be overcome by evil, but overcome evil with good" (v. 21).

Conclusion

Hopefully this book has increased your understanding of expectations. Even though in some situations you may not be conscious of your expectations, all of your expectations are important. Some of them can make a positive change in your life (make you), and some of them can have a negative impact on your life (break you).

About the Author

In 1962 Eric Jackson heard a song that would change the course of his life. While attending church with his wife in Atlanta, Georgia, he heard a blind girl sing, "If I Can Help Somebody," by A. B. Antrozzo. As the girl sang of the virtue of serving your fellow man, the words were crystallized in Eric's mind. This experience motivated him to dedicate his life to teaching God's Holy Word.

Inspired by the scripture "My people are destroyed for lack of knowledge" (Hosea 4:6, KJV), he has helped people of all ages gain knowledge and understanding of the Word of God. His teaching ministry spans more than forty-five years.

With God's guidance, Eric wrote a book in 1996, *A New Life: The Only Way to Win*. The book compares the physical and spiritual birth processes involved with salvation. It also provides limited information on becoming a Christian, Christian characteristics, choosing whom to follow, and practicing Christianity.

Eric is a native of Meherrin, Virginia, and is a graduate of Howard University and the University of Virginia. He is a retired licensed mechanical engineer. He resides with his wife, Celestine, in Newport News, Virginia. He is the father of Eric Jr., who is married to Ellen, and Cheryl, who is married to Virgil Tyler. He is the grandfather of Selena, Karina, and Virgil Jr.

Notes

Preface

1 Eric Ronald Jackson, *A New Life: The Only Way to Win*. City, Indiana: Westbrook Press, 2016, second printing.

2 Dan Reiland, "Managing Expectations as a Leader," http://danreiland.com/expectations/,

Chapter 1: Introduction

3 Dave Fleet, "Expectations Can Make or Break You," September 4, 2006, http://davefleet.com/blog/2009/04/06/expectations-make-break/

4 For more information on carnal Christians, becoming a Christian, and keys to developing Christian characteristics read:

Eric Ronald Jackson, *A New Life: The Only Way to Win*. City, Indiana: Westbrook Press, 2016, second printing.

5 The Holy Spirit is a part of the Godhead or Trinity—God the Father, God the Son (Jesus), and God the Holy Spirit, or Holy Ghost. He is not an "it" but is a person. He resides in those who have accepted Christ as their personal Savior. He bears

witness of Jesus Christ and is available to guide us, help us, comfort us, convict us of our sins, bring things to our remembrance, tell us when we are about to do things wrong (if we let Him), etc. "The fruit of the Spirit is love, joy, peace, patience, kindness, goodness, faithfulness, gentleness and self-control. Against such things there is no law" (Galatians 5:22–23 NIV).

Chapter 5: Family

6 Sheri Stritof, "Marriage Expectations: Marriage Expectations Can Make or Break a Marriage," About Relationships, http://marriage.about.com/cs/change/a/expectations.htm. Her new web site is http://widowed.about.com.

7 Livia Bardin, "*Starting Out in Mainstream America*," March 3, 2012, Available online only at http://startingout.icsa.name/